STUDIES IN THE PERSONAL SOCIAL SERVICES: NO. 3

General editors: OLIVE STEVENSON and MICHAEL HILL

SOCIAL WORK WITH ELDERLY PEOPLE

Studies in the Personal Social Services

1 SOCIAL WORK AND MONEY
by Michael Hill and Peter Laing

2 CHILD ABUSE: ASPECTS OF INTERPROFESSIONAL CO-OPERATION
by Christine Hallett and Olive Stevenson

Social Work with Elderly People

CHERRY ROWLINGS

Senior Research Fellow, Department of Social Policy and Social Work, University of Keele

London
GEORGE ALLEN & UNWIN
Boston Sydney

First published in 1981

GEORGE ALLEN & UNWIN LTD
40 Museum Street, London WC1A 1LU

British Library Cataloguing in Publication Data

Rowlings, Cherry
Social work with elderly people. – (Studies in the personal social services; no.3).
1. Geriatrics
I. Title II. Series
618.9'7'002436 80–41461

ISBN 0–04–362036–1
ISBN 0–04–362037–X Pbk

Reproduced from copy supplied
printed and bound in Great Britain
by Billing and Sons Limited
Guildford, London, Oxford, Worcester

Foreword

The main aim of this series of books on the personal social services is to shed light on key areas of concern for the organisation and practice of social work in local authorities. The books are designed for practitioners and for social work students.

The idea for a series of this kind came about from our concern to secure wider discussion of issues which arose during a study of fieldwork in social services departments. This project, funded by the Department of Health and Social Security, the Scottish Social Work Services Group and the Northern Ireland Department of Health and Social Services, was directed by Olive Stevenson and Phyllida Parsloe. Its main findings were published by HMSO in *Social Service Teams: The Practitioner's View* (DHSS, 1978). None of the books in this series directly duplicates that report, but some of the issues in them were first discussed there and some of the data quoted in them emerged from that research and may have been reported there.

One of the most significant and, from our perspective, disturbing findings in that report, which is generally confirmed by other studies and practitioners' experience, is that the elderly do not receive the amount of attention from qualified social workers that might be expected from the numbers referred to social services departments. Social services expenditure on this client group is heavy – they consume some 50 per cent of the budget allocated to residential care, home helps, meals-on-wheels and other practical services. Widespread attention is being given to the predicted increase in the numbers of the frail elderly by the end of the century which has obvious implications for social service provision.

After the main project was completed Cherry Rowlings undertook a small-scale further study of social work and the elderly in the local authority and this book draws upon and expands the material and ideas which emerged during the course of that work.

Cherry Rowlings has deliberately not entered the debate about the effectiveness of social work intervention. We know that questions are asked – are social workers necessary and do they do any good? This book is based on the assumption that if social work is good for anyone, then there can be no justification for depriving elderly people of such help. It is no part of her argument to suggest that all the elderly, or even all the elderly who come to social services departments, need continuing social work help. What she has been concerned to do is to highlight some of the skills in work with, or on behalf of, the elderly and their relatives. But, as our first report and this present study indicate, exhortations will not suffice and there is a need to experiment with a variety of approaches, in training, in professional practice and in the organisation of service. This has implications for further research.

In arguing the need to raise the level of social work service to the elderly, the author does not minimise the commitment and ability of the many – be they occupational therapists, home help organisers, or social work assistants – who in social services departments at present provide counselling and supportive help for old people. Many interviews with such staff in both our studies movingly and convincingly demonstrate their concern and their skill. But it is 'double talk' to acknowledge this and yet to back off from the problems with which some of the elderly and their relatives have to contend – problems which are just as complex and intractable as many others presented to social services.

Some examples may highlight the point. There is concern over the increasing numbers of the very elderly who show some degree of mental confusion, sometimes even severe dementia. Most of such elderly people live in the community and are dependent either on relatives living with them or nearby, or on neighbours. Whilst practical services are of great importance in reducing the strain, there is also a need for those who carry the daily stress to talk about their feelings, to express on occasion some anger and resentment, to share anxiety and to seek advice about daily management. It is part of the social worker's responsibility to see that such help is offered. It need not be the social worker who provides the help directly; that may depend on local networks of lay and professional support. It may be, for example, that groups of relatives of elderly confused clients, coming together to share some of their feelings and experiences, would be as effective in this as it has been for some relatives of the mentally handicapped. There is widespread interest in the stimulation of 'caring networks' and the social worker's role and skills in this remain to be further explored.

There is as yet little firm evidence on the emotive topic of 'granny bashing'. Respondents in Cherry Rowlings's study suggested that emotional abuse is more common than physical injury. Whilst we hope this is true, we feel that the possibility of an increase in both emotional and physical ill-treatment of the elderly is likely, given the increase in numbers of the mentally infirm, whose attitudes and behaviour can, on occasion, be provoking or intolerably distressing. It may be that there is a reluctance, comparable to that shown a decade ago by the professionals who saw children injured by their caretakers, to identify and therefore face up to a similar problem with the elderly. Without wishing to be alarmist, therefore, we see the social worker taking on more of the elements of care and surveillance that have become integral to work with children at risk. There can hardly be any aspect of social work demanding more skill.

However, that peculiarly disturbing aspect of social work with and for the elderly is but an extreme version of a wider problem, namely, that a certain number of very old people revert to emotional and physical dependence which triggers off in those who care for them powerful feelings of both tenderness and anger. As Cherry Rowlings points out, reactions to dependence are immensely varied, partly because of the individual's own personality and experience and partly because of the ways in which dependence is manifested. The point to be stressed is that the *personal* social services should be concerned with finding out what is most needed for that individual and those who care for him at that time. Whilst social workers do not have the sole prerogative of such skills, it is this individualised response which is at the heart of their training and should be integral to the mobilisation of resources as well as to the support they offer.

Since our interest in this subject was aroused and further research undertaken, the political and economic climate has changed quite dramatically. It is evident that greater emphasis will be given to the development of community support, the use of volunteers and the provisions of the voluntary sector. There is no doubt that social workers have not explored these potentialities to the full. This book concentrates (although not exclusively) on the direct relationship between social worker and client or relative. We make no apology for this since, in our view, the change of emphasis apparent at present in no way lessens the need for professional skills in the areas Cherry Rowlings discusses, which have been so little explored. Nor can we see any possibility of community and voluntary care replacing the work of social workers in social services departments. Rather we believe that the combined efforts of all these elements will scarcely suffice to meet the challenge of the numbers and needs of the frail elderly in the 1980s and beyond.

OLIVE STEVENSON
MICHAEL HILL

Acknowledgements

Many people have contributed in different ways to this book.

I am grateful to the director of Cheshire Social Services Department and the director of Devon Social Services Department for allowing me to interview staff in their departments and thereby to undertake the study which led to this book being written. I am indebted to all those who agreed to be interviewed but especially to the staff in Cheshire where most of the interviews took place. I thank them for being so ready to share their opinions and experiences.

My thanks also go to Rowena Gay, Christine Hallett, Michael Hill, Pat le Riche and Olive Stevenson for their very helpful comments on the first draft. Olive Stevenson and Michael Hill have also, as editors, offered much-needed encouragement and constructive advice and I am grateful to them.

Finally, Jill Phillips and Janet Wilson have shared the typing and I thank them both for doing this with such willingness and good humour.

CHERRY ROWLINGS

To my parents

Contents

Introduction

Old age is not necessarily a time of problems; many elderly people and their families will not require assistance from a social worker nor indeed from any other outside helper. Other elderly people will require domiciliary services or maybe aids to daily living but this need for social *service* does not in itself indicate a need for social work. Some elderly people, however, experience problems of an inter- or intrapersonal nature which, by virtue of complexity or severity, seem an appropriate area of work for a qualified social worker. It is with this last group of elderly people and at times also their families that this book is largely concerned.

Social work with elderly people is a subject which hitherto has not excited much professional interest and concern. Although there are signs that this may be changing, it is still true that social workers generally have less understanding of old age and of the problems that may be encountered by elderly people than they have of the experience of childhood, for example. Furthermore, whilst elderly people consume a significant proportion of the local authority expenditure devoted to social services provision – in 1977/8, 20 per cent of the total net social services expenditure in England and Wales was spent on residential care for elderly people (CIPFA, 1979) – qualified social workers spend a very small proportion of their time on the problems of old age. There are, of course, exceptions, notably in the hospital setting, but the general pattern of case allocation and of caseload composition in area teams has been clearly described in several recent studies (Holme and Maizels, 1978; DHSS, 1978; Goldberg *et al.*, 1978). These demonstrate just how widespread is the practice whereby, in teams consisting of a mix of qualified and unqualified staff and maybe a trainee and one or more social work assistants, the qualified staff work predominately with cases involving children and the assistants and other unqualified staff are largely and at times exclusively involved with elderly clients.

The reasons for this division of labour are complex and are discussed in more detail in the following chapter. Here, it is sufficient to comment that whilst it is true that social work has still to achieve the difficult task of defining appropriate areas of work, the almost total exclusion of the problems of elderly people from social work caseloads suggests that the current criteria for allocating social work time can only be described as crude. For, as later chapters will demonstrate, there is no evidence that as people become older, so their problems become less severe or less complex or that their coping mechanisms become more developed.

One of the main aims of this book is to encourage a heightened awareness amongst social workers of the problems facing some elderly people and to promote discussion about the nature of social work with elderly clients and the occasions when intervention by a qualified social worker is appropriate and when it is not. The deployment of staff with different levels and types of training in social services departments is an issue of crucial importance and has particular relevance to provision for elderly clients, where at maybe one and the same time different contributions are required from a home help, occupational therapist, social worker and perhaps also from others outside the agency such as district nurse or voluntary visitor.

Thus, to focus on the need to develop the role of the qualified social worker in relation to elderly clients is not to undervalue the work of the unqualified and ancillary staff who currently provide the major part of the care and support offered to elderly clients; nor is it to deny the high level of sensitivity, intuitive skill and experience which many bring to their work. Rather, it is to suggest that there are some – but by no means all – elderly clients whose problems place upon the worker responsibilities and demands which it is appropriate to expect qualified staff to handle. If it is accepted that work which is more difficult, more stressful and which involves a high degree of responsibility for the future well-being of the client should rightly be handled by qualified staff – as is often argued to support the continued involvement of qualified staff in work with children – then it is difficult to uphold the continuation of a system in which staff who are without training and who are in junior or ancillary posts are nevertheless the only workers directly involved in cases where there is a high degree of risk, of family dysfunction, of mental frailty, or emotional disturbance.

There are two additional reasons why this author believes that it is urgent for trained social workers to clarify their role with elderly clients. The first is that the development of the Certificate in Social Service (CSS) as an alternative form of training to the Certificate of Qualification in Social Work (CQSW) requires the roles of CSS and the CQSW staff to be more clearly defined – if, that is, staff are to be appropriately deployed. Secondly, following the social workers' strike in the winter of 1978/9, local settlements have emphasised that certain tasks and responsibilities should be allocated to staff according to their level of training and of experience. At the time of writing it is too soon to assess how these settlements and the employment of CSS staff are affecting the allocation of work and, in particular, the response to referrals on elderly clients. Potentially, however, the repercussions could be far-reaching. The development in CSS training of options in work with elderly clients could result in the CSS being seen as the training for work with that client group. Additionally, if work with elderly clients continues to be regarded as innately less difficult, then the terms of the local settlements are unlikely significantly to alter existing allocation procedures in relation to elderly clients. Both these possibilities could become reality if CQSW staff fail either to increase their knowledge and understanding of the problems experienced by some elderly people or to recognise where the complexity of the problem requires the involvement of a worker with the type of qualification that is provided by CQSW training.

NOTE

Throughout the book, considerable use is made of case illustrations and of social workers' accounts of their work with elderly clients. This material comes from a study funded by the DHSS which the author undertook (Rowlings, 1978) in order to explore the needs of elderly people and to consider the role of the social worker as one element in the provision of service to the elderly clients of social services departments. In the study a deliberate decision was taken to seek out examples of practice from social workers, all of whom had some training in social work or in counselling, who were working largely or exclusively with elderly clients. The intention was to explore practice and ideas with these workers in the hope that their experiences would contribute to a greater understanding of the nature of social work with elderly clients. Unless otherwise stated, the opinions and case examples quoted in this book come from the interviews with the social work and social service staff who participated in the study.

Chapter 1

'... And Third the Elderly'

This chapter may be seen as a background to the rest of the book, in that it explores social workers' attitudes towards elderly people and considers some of the reasons why it may not be easy for social workers to face problems presented by the old.

In contemporary society which is oriented towards the young, attitudes towards the old can best be described as ambivalent. Butler (1974) identified six widely held images or myths of old age which assume that ageing is a uniform process – for example, that all old people are unproductive, inflexible and are or will become forgetful, confused and inattentive. An alternative, more attractive myth is that of old age as a time of serenity; people live 'in a kind of adult fairyland' of peace, relaxation and contentment (p. 532). The existence of these myths has been interpreted by Butler and also by de Beauvoir (1972), in her treatise on old age, as the mechanism by which the young may divorce and thereby protect themselves from facing the experiences of those older than themselves.

One of the important features of these myths is their failure to differentiate and to individualise the process of ageing. A similar phenomenon can be found in some attitudes expressed about the needs of elderly people seeking help from social services departments. As a group, they may be perceived as having problems that are predominately straightforward and therefore susceptible to help administered according to routine procedures (DHSS, 1978, p. 143): 'The assistants get the sort of cases involving gas or electricity accounts because there are set procedures for dealing with them. *I think there is also a pattern for dealing with the elderly in the same way*' (author's italics). Moreover, events regarded as potentially stressful for children may be viewed as being intrinsically less significant for a person near the end of his life: 'An elderly person has fewer years and it doesn't have as big an effect on an old person going into an old people's home as it does on a child going into a children's home.'

Comments such as these illustrate the existence of certain stereotypes about elderly clients which emphasise the low status of this section of the client population. Brearley (1975) has noted the prevalence of adjectives with negative connotations to describe social work with elderly clients – 'difficult', 'slow', 'limited', and so on. Social work is not, of course, the only profession which shares a predominately negative view of old age; geriatric nursing and geriatric medicine, for example, are not widely regarded as interesting or prestigious specialisms. Kosberg and Harris (1978) quote several American studies which found social workers, nurses and psychiatrists sharing a view of work with elderly clients as boring and with little prospect of reward or satisfaction for the worker. One study found that the attitudes of a group of medical students demonstrated greater prejudice against old age than against race. Indeed, the term 'agism' has become accepted as indicating prejudice or discrimination against people on account of their age.

Thus, the definition of priority for social work attention in social services – 'first child care, second mental health and third the elderly' (DHSS, 1978, p. 142) – reflects both the primacy accorded to children and the lowly position occupied by clients who are old. It is worth noting that this 'pecking order' corresponds closely to the likes and dislikes of a group of CQSW students who were asked during and after their training to indicate whether or not they enjoyed working with certain clients or problems. Work with families and children emerged as very popular, with 88 per cent of the students answering in the affirmative. Work with mentally ill clients was liked by 66 per cent of the students, making this the second most popular focus of work, and cases involving fostering and adoption came close behind (63 per cent). But three client groups – those who were mentally handicapped (34 per cent), who were sick and disabled (31 per cent) and who were elderly (28 per cent) – received far and away the lowest number of positive responses (DHSS, 1978).

The popularity of child care work is to be expected in a society that is child oriented. It is also not surprising given the manner in which local authority social work has developed as a profession largely in response to the legislation about the care to be made available to children and their families. Further evidence of the importance attached to the care of children can be seen in the Acts of Parliament that, particularly since 1948, have imposed wide-ranging powers, duties and responsibilities upon local authorities in respect of children. This contrasts with the comparatively small amount of legislation passed in relation to mentally ill people or those who are disabled or old and which in addition is generally more permissive than that relating to children.

It is perhaps as a consequence of this difference in the amount and type of legislation that the expression 'statutory work' is rapidly becoming synonymous with work with children (although, as agencies established by statute, all the activities of social services departments can be described as 'statutory'). Moreover, although none of the laws or regulations governing care of children specifies whether the worker involved should be trained or untrained, experienced or inexperienced, social worker or ancillary, there is an underlying assumption that 'statutory work' should rightly be handled by qualified social workers. It can, therefore, be seen that the public and professional concern and anxiety which understandably exists in relation to the prevention and detection of child abuse has heightened, but not in itself created an atmosphere in which work with children is viewed as inherently more complex and with a greater potential for damage or distress to the client.

But to return specifically to attitudes towards old age: it is evident that stereotypes and assumptions about ageing and people who have grown old may contribute towards the allocation of social work time primarily in the direction of children. There is, however, a second dimension to be considered – namely, how social workers who have elderly clients approach the problems that are presented. Several writers (Wasser, 1966; Cormican, 1977; Kosberg and Harris, 1978) have commented on the failure or reluctance of social workers to take on an active role with their elderly clients. Goldberg *et al.* (1978) noted that in the area team they studied the social workers described most of their work with elderly clients as preservation or maintenance of the status quo. They rarely described their aims as directed towards emotional problems or the modification of behaviour, attitudes or environment. The researchers ask (p. 259): 'Does this convey a stoic acceptance by social workers of the status quo among the elderly or a failure to appreciate how much the appropriate kind of emotional or practical support at the right time can contribute to a more easeful life of the very old?'

Kosberg and Harris suggest that in general social workers accept the adverse conditions of old age rather than seek to change them. They point out that, for example, many social workers have for some time been critical of the environment in some residential homes or long-stay hospitals. Yet few have attempted to bring about change in these institutions, even though they have continued to refer clients for permanent care. It is known that many elderly people have a fatalistic and even pessimistic approach to the difficulties they may experience in old age. Their expectation that problems are 'normal' and are irremediable is summed up in the remark 'It's just old age', which often serves both to explain problems and to discourage attempts to find a solution. Do social workers hold back from seeking change or amelioration because they share this fatalism?

It may be, as Clare Winnicott (1964) suggested in relation to 'face to face' work with children, that social workers hold back because they feel ill-equipped to confront the apparently overwhelming needs of the clients, the extent of the suffering some experience and the difficult decisions about how 'deep' they, the workers, should go. These three reasons are, of course, related; decisions about the 'depth' of involvement depend not just on the client's capacity to be helped thus (a point of particular importance, if the client is mentally or physically very frail) but also on the social worker's confidence that he will be able to cope professionally and personally with the strength of feelings that may be released.

The strength of feelings experienced by some elderly people is described in the following chapter which considers some of the challenges that face elderly people. The purpose here is to focus on the response of social workers, and indeed of many people in society, to the prospect of ageing and the significance of that future stage of life for them.

Involvement with elderly people confronts those who are young with man's mortality. This may, in a subtle way, be different from the contact with death that is an inevitable part of being with a young person who is terminally ill. For as Soyer (1969, p. 292) wrote: 'The death of a younger man may be far more tragic; yet it is less inevitable. It does not underscore man's mortality, for its very tragedy is in the fact that the younger person *might have* lived. The decline and death of the older person reminds us that this must eventually happen to all' (italics in original). In order to deny and avoid this, the young may seek comfort in emphasising the extraordinary achievements of some older people – the 80-year-old woman who regularly takes strenuous exercise or the aged musician or statesman whose faculties, energy and creativity continue to flourish. The media are full of such examples; at the time of writing, much attention was being given to an energetic centenarian whose wish to fly in Concorde had been fulfilled.

It is significant that Soyer emphasises that old age confronts us not just with death (which is inevitable) but with decline (which is probable, at least to some degree). Indeed, as more people survive into their eighties and nineties, so more will experience mental and/or physical frailty before death. It may well be that this aspect of ageing causes more alarm or anxiety than the certainty of death: it is the prospect of loss in old age – impairment in mental and/or physical function, loss of spouse and family and loss of independence – which is more frightening to contemplate than loss of life itself.

Many of the elderly people who come to social services departments are experiencing or have recently experienced significant loss. They may ask the question outright 'What have I got to live for now?' and it may be hard for the worker to identify any positives. It is not easy to be with people who seem dominated by a sense of uselessness or shaken by grief or loneliness, perhaps of a kind which has aroused in them powerful emotions of which they were previously unaware. Nor is it easy to face that such loss and pain may be experienced by our friends, our families and ourselves. The very experience of someone else's pain will evoke a powerful response, as Leared (1978, p. 17) has pointed out: 'If someone is mourning the loss of some capacity, home, independence, a limb or sight, we in our imagination are in touch with some loss of capacity we fear for ourselves.'

These are very powerful reasons why social workers may have difficulty in being 'open' to the experiences of those elderly clients for whom ageing is a period of their life far removed from the peace and contentment of the myth. The implications of 'normal' ageing are not easy for young or old to face and the possibilities of loneliness, of physical and mental impairment and, perhaps above all, of dependency confront us with questions about how we wish to age and what we fear for our own old age. Social workers may well be faced with clients whose experience of and response to ageing represents those very aspects of old age which they, the social workers, fear most for their future selves.

Yet it can be argued that these same aspects of ageing constitute what should be a main concern of social workers. Morris (1977, p. 353) advocates that 'the core of social work development' lies in the assumption of responsibility for the provision of care for those in the population who depend on others for their survival. The management of dependency is a major task for those who require care and those who provide it – a point elaborated in the following chapter. Morris suggests that direct caring *for* people rather than caring *about* them is work for which the ethics and the knowledge base of social work are particularly applicable and necessary. Moreover, a focus such as this would provide social work with a clearer identity than it has now and would encourage its development as a profession with a leading role in the field of health and social welfare.

Soyer (1969) offers a personal view of the significance of working with elderly people, suggesting that it gives expression to the core values of social work, most particularly that of the intrinsic value of each human being (p. 292): 'working with the aged ... gives the worker a chance to test temper and affirm this core value of our profession'. He also believes (p. 294) that working with elderly people offers a perspective which because it looks back over a life, rather than forward, 'can broaden one's sensitivity to the full range of human experience'. In a later chapter, the value of reminiscence is discussed from the point of view of the elderly person; Soyer reminds us here that listening to reminiscence is not without value for the personal and the professional development of the worker.

This chapter has focused on the reasons why the problems of the old may evoke a different response from social workers than do the problems of the young. The following chapter describes what is known of the circumstances of elderly people in Britain today and considers how the knowledge about certain experiences in old age may be important for social workers.

Chapter 2

Social Work and the Problems of Elderly People

In 1951, the population of Great Britain totalled 49·2 million; of these, 6,662,000 (13·6 per cent) were people over retiring age. By 1977, the estimated total population had risen to 54·4 million, with people of pensionable age numbering 9,419,000 or 17·3 per cent.* These figures are evidence of a dramatic change in the balance of the population over a comparatively short space of time, and reflect the advances in environmental health, preventive medicine and the treatment of disease that have taken place throughout the century. Considerably more young children can now expect to reach old age than was the case at the beginning of the century, as Table 2.1 demonstrates (OPCS, 1979, table 82). The figures relate to Great Britain.

Table 2.1 *Life expectancy*

	Males				*Females*			
	1901	*1931*	*1961*	*1975*	*1901*	*1931*	*1961*	*1975*
Further number of years which a person can expect to live:								
at birth	48·1	58·4	67·9	69·4	51·8	62·5	73·8	75·6
at age 1 year	55·1	62·1	68·6	69·6	57·6	65·2	74·2	75·6
5 years	55·5	60·0	64·9	65·8	58·0	63·0	70·5	71·7
30 years	34·5	38·1	40·9	41·7	37·1	41·0	46·1	47·2
45 years	23·1	25·5	26·9	27·6	25·4	28·2	31·9	32·9
60 years	13·4	14·4	15·0	15·5	14·9	16·4	19·0	20·1
70 years	8·4	8·6	9·3	9·5	9·2	10·0	11·7	12·6
80 years	4·9	4·7	5·2	5·4	5·3	5·5	6·3	6·9

* Readers in Northern Ireland should note that these figures are not directly applicable to the Province, where a smaller proportion of the population is elderly.

Between 1977 and the end of the century, and assuming that mortality rates are not affected by a major unforeseen disaster, two distinct trends will be evident in the population over retiring age. First, the overall proportion of old people will continue to rise until the mid-1980s, when it will reach a peak of 18 per cent of the total population, and then fall to 17.7 per cent in 1991, rising again in the early 2000s – a pattern which reflects the low birth rate of the interwar years and the higher rate which followed the end of the Second World War.

Secondly, and of equal if not more importance, is that the profile of the elderly population itself is changing. Within the wide age-span described as 'elderly', the most significant increases are occurring in the number of the 'old' old – those aged 75 and over – and the 'oldest' old – those aged 85 and over. This is well illustrated in Table 2.2 (OPCS, 1978), which shows that the numbers of very old people (75 and over) will rise proportionately considerably more than those who are the 'young' old.

Table 2.2 *Profile of the elderly population*

Age-group	*1975*	*1981*	*2001*	*Percentage change 1975–2001*
60–64	3,178,000	2,931,000	2,735,000	– 13·9
65–69	2,831,000	2,759,000	2,411,000	– 14·8
70–74	2,213,000	2,345,000	2,137,000	– 3·4
75–79	1,447,000	1,664,000	1,733,000	+ 19·8
80–84	822,000	936,000	1,075,000	+ 30·8
85 and over	515,000	550,000	752,000	+ 46·3
Whole population (all ages)	56,043,000	55,911,000	58,345,000	+ 4·1

Women far outnumber men in this very old group, a reflection in part of the longevity of women and the depletion of the male population in the two world wars. Many elderly women are without a spouse, either because they have never married or because they are widowed (65 per cent of women aged 75 and over in 1974 were widows). A proportion will also be without children, because of childlessness or because their children have died. In a survey of old people aged 70 and over in four English towns (Abrams, 1978a), 30 per cent of the respondents had never had children and another 5 per cent had outlived their offspring. These figures raise several important questions. As a general point, one may speculate about the significance of this numerical inequality of the sexes (women aged 75–84 outnumber men in the same age-group by more than two to one); to what extent are many of the problems of elderly people (low income, subordinate status in society, etc.) the problems of *women*, irrespective of their age? Of more direct relevance to social services departments and to health authorities, however, is the development of social and emotional supports that may be necessary as substitutes for the caring role normally provided by spouse and by family, especially adult children. And not least to be considered are the needs of elderly men in a predominately female peer-group, a point which requires special thought in the organisation of residential and day care establishments where not only the residents but also the staff are likely to be female.

The process of growing old involves changes that take place over time, at varying speeds and on several dimensions. These will not necessarily occur at the same time as each other; a newly retired man, receiving his 'old' age pension, may have difficulty in accepting this social definition of himself as aged when his interests, state of health and life-style have far more in common with those of a younger rather than an older age-group. The whole process of ageing is a highly individual one which as yet has received less attention than the physical and psychological development of children. One of the difficulties facing social workers is that 'normal' ageing is less well understood than 'normal' child development, where stages of physical, intellectual and moral development have been charted alongside chronological age. Such information may provide the social worker with guidelines in his direct work with children, for instance, if this involves discussions about separation or about the death of a parent. The age of an elderly client provides no such guide to physical capacity, comprehension and understanding; indeed, Rapoport *et al.* (1977, p. 321) conclude from their studies that 'the variation among individuals increases as the age of the people increases'.

Although it is essential, therefore, to recognise that there will be wide differences within and between the different age-groups that are categorised as 'elderly', it is also important to accept the fact that *most* old people will experience *some* degree of frailty before they die, and the longer they survive into old age, the more likely it is that their life will be restricted by some loss of function and by the absence of spouse, siblings, friends and maybe also children.

Recent studies of the characteristics and the needs of the elderly population illustrate that the age of 75 can be regarded as a point at which the consequences of ageing begin to be most clearly visible. Hunt (1978), writing of her survey of old people aged 65 and over living in the community in England in 1976, summarises her findings thus (pp. 4–5):

> physically, the 65–74 year olds are, for the most part, not much more severely disadvantaged than the age group immediately below their own ... They appear at least as likely as younger people to have hobbies, interests and social contacts. Many say categorically they do not consider themselves to be elderly ... Their housing conditions and amenities are, in general, not greatly inferior to those of younger people.

But she continues:

> The 75–84 age group shows a moderate decline in some things: mobility, health, ability to perform personal and domestic tasks, favourable attitudes to life. In other things there is a much sharper decline: in social contacts outside the home, in having hobbies and in living alone. Their standards of housing and amenities on average are lower. Among those aged 85 and over, virtually all these trends are accelerated.

Isaacs and Neville (1976), in their study of the medical and social needs of old people in three areas of Scotland, also noted the significance of age (p. 12):

> potential need was a strongly age-related phenomenon, increasing in frequency and severity with increasing age of subject. It was largely independent of all other variables studied ... The association between age and potential need was highly significant for all types of need.

Not only are the very old more likely to require frequent

domiciliary services but several different services may be necessary – health visitor and/or home nursing, home help and meals-on-wheels all providing regular support in addition to periodic visits by a social work assistant or social worker (Avon, 1977). Figures on bed occupancy in psychiatric and general hospitals show that people over the age of 75 are major consumers of in-patient hospital care; although constituting some 5 per cent of the population, they occupy around 22 per cent of the beds in these hospitals (DHSS, 1976, 1977). Thus the projected increase in the population over 75, which, unlike the future birth rate, can be reliably predicted, is a matter of great importance for those who plan and provide health and welfare services.

It is to be expected that increasing age is generally accompanied by increasing frailty and this normal process of diminution and decline sometimes may be accelerated by illness or injury. This forms part of the context of work with elderly people and indicates the importance for social workers to be alert to the increased possibility of multiple medical and social need amongst people who are very old. It is, however, equally important to put the needs of many elderly people into a wider perspective. Old age *per se* is not the primary problem of all old people. Many of the problems that they may experience are consequent upon or exacerbated by low income, poor housing, unemployment, bereavement, ill-health and disability which, while they may be more prevalent amongst those aged 65 and over, are certainly not unique to that age-group.

Nor is it easy to determine whether it is old age or some of its unwelcome accompaniments which explain the social and psychological state of elderly people. An influential study on ageing (Cumming and Henry, 1961) suggested that the normal process by which old people adjust to ageing is through a gradual disengagement from society and a narrowing of their range of interests, friends, activities, and so on. As a theory of *ageing*, this has been widely criticised because it failed to take sufficient account of the unavoidable circumstances in which many elderly people may be placed – for example, the absence of employment. Hochschild (in Gubrium, 1976) quotes a study which showed that young men in long-term unemployment came to display a passivity and a decreasing interest in life and the world around them similar to the state of disengagement which Cumming and Henry had attributed to the ageing process. Or, to take the example of bereavement: the dislocation caused by widowhood is not confined to the young and may involve a considerable and often unwelcome change in the life-style of an elderly person who has been accustomed to thirty or more years of shared living, eating and sleeping (Tunstall, 1966).

It is relevant, therefore, to consider the problems which face many elderly people and which may at some stage form part of the focus of social work help. Although a number of themes could have been selected – the effects of retirement, for example, or of the status of old people in present-day society – four have been chosen as having a particular relevance for the role of the social worker. These are poverty amongst the old; dependency; bereavement, loss and isolation; and mental infirmity.

POVERTY AMONGST THE OLD

The association between old age and poverty, as defined by the level of supplementary benefit (SB), is by now well established. Layard *et al.* (1978), writing a background paper for the Royal Commission on the Distribution of Income and Wealth, made the point succinctly (p. 114): 'More than half the poor are elderly ... A half of the elderly are living close to the SB level.'

Pensioners are the largest single group of claimants of supplementary benefit (in the form of supplementary pensions) – 58 per cent of the total number of claimants in 1977 (Report of the Supplementary Benefits Commission, 1978). It is estimated that about a quarter (26 per cent) of old people who would be entitled to receive a supplementary pension do not, in fact, apply; perhaps because of ignorance of what is available, a dislike of the stigma, as they perceive it, of receiving charity, or resignation to a limited standard of living. Although the Social Security Act 1975 should make some improvement to the basic income of pensioners after the turn of the century, it seems that the position of pensions relative to current earnings is unlikely to be much affected (Bosanquet, 1978).

Another aspect of the poverty of old people can be found when comparing their housing and their amenities with those of the rest of the population. Again, this is complicated by the expectations of old people: washing machines or fridges, for example, were not part of their youth and may therefore not be wanted or they may be regarded with some suspicion. But leaving aside the comparatively low level of possession of consumer durables to be found amongst the elderly population, the standard of housing occupied by a significant number of elderly people is a cause for concern. Very old houses may well be occupied by very old people; this increases the likelihood of an outside lavatory, no running hot water, inadequate forms of heating and poor insulation. Although just over 40 per cent of the elderly population in England own their house this does not mean that the owner-occupiers necessarily have an easier time; the ongoing cost of the upkeep of the property may be prohibitive for elderly persons on a minimum income and those who receive a supplementary pension may be unaware that it is possible to claim an Exceptional Needs Payment for major repairs (Age Concern, 1974; Bosanquet, 1978).

The prevalence of poverty amongst the old – and the oldest also tend to be the poorest – indicates that many old people are perforce dependent on public sector services if they require assistance in daily living; to buy in private domestic help or to purchase private chiropody, for example, is beyond their means. When the private market is unavailable, the impact of restricted growth or cuts in social service expenditure must be severe; indeed, at the time of writing the press has contained a number of accounts of closure of old people's homes, cuts in the budget for home helps and the like. And this at a time when that section of the elderly population known to be likely to need help (that is, those aged over 75) is increasing both numerically and proportionately.

The relatively impoverished standard of living experienced by many elderly people has considerable significance (both actual and potential) for the role of the social worker. At a general level, it may be argued that it is part of the function of social workers 'not to remain silent when they know that [material] needs are not being met, or being inadequately met' (Younghusband, 1964, p. 107). Since it is in the nature of things that resources are normally made available only after need has been proved to exist, it is important that unmet or partially met need does not pass unrecorded.

However, on an individual level social workers may be involved with clients who have a notion of wealth and of adequacy which differs markedly from contemporary standards. The experiences of economic stringency during both world wars and the years of the Depression will have accustomed many elderly people to life on an income which requires the most careful management. Such habits have often become firmly ingrained; old people may be proud of their ability to 'manage', to keep themselves out of debt and to avoid charity and may thus be prepared to accept a restricted and maybe inadequate diet or a low room temperature. A lifetime of saving continues and it may be difficult to persuade an elderly person to spend the money he has to make his life more comfortable. A home help organiser said: 'They say they're saving for a rainy day but they don't seem to realise that their rainy day has come. Although they may have no one to leave the money to, they like the assurance they they have the bank book with money in ...' The saving may be for a 'decent' burial – and given the smallness of the death grant, the money may indeed be necessary if the burial is to achieve this level of respectability.

Yet although some old people may be reluctant or even opposed to accepting material help, there is no doubt that the provision of such help forms an important part of social work with old people (Wasser, 1966; Goldberg *et al.*, 1970). The significance of material aid is clearly considerable, and this is to be expected in that it may make an immediate and possibly appreciable difference to the life of someone on a low income. Moreover, it is a form of assistance which is readily and easily identifiable by both worker and client – and it is also remembered. In his study of social work with young families in contact with a voluntary social work agency, Sainsbury (1975) found that mothers remembered with warm appreciation the material help offered by social workers; the comments in the study by Goldberg *et al.* (1970) show that elderly clients may be no less appreciative. Although intervention which results in a more comfortable life for the client should be valued in its own right (and not just as the means of establishing a relationship with the client), for some clients material help clearly represents something 'extra' – proof, perhaps of someone's concern and interest. This may be particularly important for clients who have few opportunities to experience being within a caring relationship. An officer-in-charge observed: 'practical services and material aid are the outward sign that they are going to get help – talk is cheap, as they say, but when you *do* send in some help, that shows something'.

In most of the accounts of the benefits of material assistance to elderly clients, one subject has been largely overlooked – namely, the role of social workers as advocates and arbitrators in the allocation of resources. The extent to which social workers should be involved in advocacy and welfare rights has been discussed largely in relation to their powers under section 1 of the Children and Young Persons Act 1963 or under the equivalent but more broadly defined powers incorporated within section 12 of the Social Work (Scotland) Act 1968; (this allows assistance in kind or in cash to be given, irrespective of the age of the client, if it can be shown that such help decreases the likelihood that the department will be required to intervene in the future). Except where social workers are employed in the Scottish social work departments or where they have access to hospital Samaritan or League of Friends funds, the question of providing elderly clients with financial assistance does not, of course, arise. However, even without the financial powers that they have in relation to children, social workers with elderly clients are in a potentially powerful position over the allocation of services and resources from within their own department – home help hours, day care and residential care places, for example – and may have some influence over the allocation of the resources of other departments and agencies – notably housing departments and supplementary benefits. In addition, they can refer their clients to the various voluntary and charitable organisations which between them provide a variety of services including sheltered accommodation, residential care, 'friendly visitors' and financial aid. Given the complexity of benefits, services and resources available from the many statutory and voluntary agencies which have some responsibility for elderly people, it is likely that many, probably most, elderly clients will be at a disadvantage in knowing both what is available and from which agency or department.

But the availability of options does not in itself mean that choice is limitless or unrestricted, with the result that the bargaining or 'brokerage' skills of the social worker assume considerable importance if the client is to receive the quality of help that is required. The power of the social worker comes both from his knowledge of what is available and from his ability to put forward the client's case; and skill in the latter may assume particular importance when there are many competing demands upon already overstretched resources. Shanas and Sussman (1977) have argued that social workers should develop the roles of advocate and organiser, leaving the provision of 'affective and emotional' supports to family networks or less highly trained people. This would allow social workers to concentrate on the complex task of facilitating the linkages between welfare organisations and old people and their families; of enabling them to make appropriate and successful contact with bureaucratic organisations (both voluntary and statutory); and of ensuring that the organisations are receptive and responsive to the needs of the people whom they serve.

Other writers have argued the need for social workers to achieve competence in the areas of advocacy and welfare rights (Wootton, 1959; Sinfield, 1969). Hill and Laing (1978, 1979) discuss this issue as it relates to social workers and the use of money under section 1 of the 1963 Children and Young Persons Act. They acknowledge in full the importance of the tasks of offering advice, advocacy and representation, but question (Hill and Laing, 1978, p. 49) whether these are necessarily appropriate for social workers: 'perhaps [social workers] should have been more ready to argue that, while these are vital tasks which should be performed by someone, they are not intrinsically social work tasks'.

This point is of equal relevance for social workers with elderly clients. A good deal of publicity and education can be appropriately and successfully provided not by social workers but by voluntary agencies which can raise the level of awareness in the public as a whole and amongst those elderly people who are able to put forward their own views and requests once they know what might be available and from which organisation or department. Age Concern, for example, provides information and advice on matters concerning pensions, supplementary benefits and income tax. If an elderly person does not have the necessary level of expertise or has been unsuccessful in his preliminary attempts to put his case, it is by no means proven that the advice or advocacy required is of a kind that should be provided by a social worker. A thorough knowledge of welfare rights legislation and of the resources available in the statutory and voluntary sectors may indeed constitute a specialism in its own right, but one which is distinct from social work even though it may be located within welfare organisations.

This leaves a third group of elderly people with whom social workers would be involved, because the nature of the resource required (long-term care, for example) or additional difficulties experienced by the client (such as depression or interpersonal problems) makes it appropriate for social work rather than non-social work staff to be in contact with the client. The depth and complexity of the social and emotional problems of some elderly people and their families suggests that, contrary to the assertion by Shanas and Sussman, better-trained rather than less-trained staff are required. However, whilst the skills of the social worker may be necessary in order to undertake direct work with the client, it may be that the task of actually acquiring the resource required, or of advising about what is available, is the responsibility of a worker who specialises in this field and who is familiar with the multiplicity of options available through the statutory and the voluntary agencies.

Thus the time is right for the debates about the place of advice, assistance and advocacy that centre on the powers under section 1 of the 1963 Children and Young Persons Act to adopt a broader focus and include the equivalent activities on behalf of elderly clients and indeed others who, for whatever reason, are severely disadvantaged in articulating their need for benefit or services.

DEPENDENCY

This section and the following one on loss are closely linked, for many elderly people are faced with a diminution and at times a considerable loss of independence, on a scale which they are unlikely to have experienced since childhood, and they may indeed grieve for their previous physical and mental agility.

Little information exists to describe the process by which a person with a history of coping and of activity comes to terms with increasing dependency on others for various aspects of daily living. It may be that since some dependency is not uncommon in old age, this makes it easier to accept, but the determination to manage and the pride in coping that is exhibited by many elderly people suggests that this is unlikely. And it is not unusual for those who have become unable to cope adequately on their own to take pains to emphasise that they have not always been 'like this' and to describe their past achievements as proof of better days.

In old age, the extent and duration of dependency are far less certain than they are in childhood. An old person may come to require as much care and protection as a young child or hardly any at all; he may be minimally dependent on others for many years or for only a few; and this may or may not be followed by a period of extreme dependency. The uncertainty about what the future holds may itself be a cause for anxiety to both the old person and his caretakers and may, for example, prompt him to seek some form of 'insurance' through asking to be put on a waiting list for residential care.

A number of factors will affect an individual's response to the experience of being dependent. It may be that the loss of the accustomed extent of independence is in itself of prime importance, irrespective of the form it takes, because self-sufficiency and physical health and strength are the means by which a person expresses himself. Paradoxically, the inability to face dependency is perhaps one of the greatest threats to the preservation of remaining independence, since the provision of an appropriate level of care and support is the means by which the gap between actual and potential function is narrowed (Brody, 1977b). But elderly people who steadfastly refuse any form of assistance are but a small minority and most will adjust to dependency in a way which demonstrates that whilst the extent and the nature of the dependency is important, so also is the significance of the activity no longer possible.

Thus, relying on others to do the gardening is likely to matter more to a person who has always been an enthusiastic gardener than it will to one who has regarded gardening as an unwelcome chore. Some restrictions on life are generally more acceptable and easier to manage than others and may, therefore, pose less of a threat to dignity and integrity; for example, help with shopping is probably easier for the helper to provide and for the dependent person to accept than is assistance to get to the lavatory. It is also possible to partialise certain activities which can be no longer carried out in full and it may be that, for example, the inability to go shopping is tolerable so long as the elderly person writes the shopping list of the vegetables and groceries to be bought. In working with people who are becoming less able to care for themselves, it is vital to identify the everyday things which are for them the most important expressions of themselves and then to find a way either of safeguarding these or of choosing the closest alternative so that they are not stripped of involvement in the management of their daily life.

The experience of dependency has been analysed mostly in relation to young adults for whom disability or frailty is unusual. The strong and conflicting emotions that are evoked by the state of dependency are not all at a conscious level. There will be anger, frustration and sorrow at being less capable than previously; insecurity because of the loss of control over some aspect of one's life; enjoyment of and gratitude for the care one receives; impatience and anger when the care seems inadequate; envy of the capabilities of the carer; and guilt at these angry feelings towards the caring persons. The more significant the dependency, the more likely it is that the dependent person will experience feelings of helplessness, vulnerability and dread of abandonment such as are part of early childhood (Klein, 1959; Rochlin, 1965).

Although we lack accounts by an elderly person which are comparable to the material of Ritchie (1960), which increased our understanding of how a person copes with the aftermath of a stroke, it is important that we are open to the significance of dependency for elderly people. This is not to suggest that all dependent elderly people will experience the range and intensity of ambivalent feelings outlined in the previous paragraph. Given the present state of knowledge it is impossible to say with certainty. But an elderly person who becomes less able to look after himself is faced with a new and changing image of himself which perhaps shows him that he is no longer growing old – he *is* old. The world and his place in it may no longer seem so safe and certain as he copes both with his own physical limitations and with the status of being old in contemporary society which threatens individual identity. The following quotations come from two members of a group of residents in an American nursing home (Harris, 1979, p. 159):

> Yes I feel weak, unsure of my footing, but I don't feel old and I don't like being stereotyped. I do not live in the past and I'm not afraid of the future.

and

> I don't want to be stereotyped as an old person. I'm me.

Similar sentiments are voiced in the title of the article 'I'm not poor, I'm not old and I'm not her dear' (Worth, 1975) and in the anonymous poem in *Community Care* (no. 178, p. 22) which was written by an elderly patient and discovered in her locker when it was cleared out after her death. The poem begins with a question 'What do you see, nurses, what do you see?' and ends with an urgent plea:

> Open your eyes, nurses, open and see
> Not a crabbit old woman, look closer – See ME!

The experience of dependency involves new kinds of relationships which may encroach on aspects of living previously regarded as private. These relationships may be with adult children who now take on parenting functions in respect of their parents. This role reversal calls for considerable adjustment on both sides and the form it takes may well depend on the quality of the parenting which the now adult child experienced when young. A boy who blamed his father for an unhappy childhood or a girl who witnessed her father abusing her mother may, as adults, be unable to offer the elderly man care and protection. And for the elderly person himself, his memories of how he treated *his* parents influence his expectations or demands of how he should be treated by his children. Some of these complex three- or four-generational family relationships are explored in a later chapter.

The experience of being depended upon evokes a range of feelings not dissimilar in kind from those of the person who is receiving care. A study of the stress experienced by nurses (Menzies, 1960) showed that while nurses felt compassion for their patients, they also experienced anxiety at being confronted with suffering and death – an anxiety which in turn produced feelings of guilt, of resentment against the patients who provoked these feelings and of envy of the care they received. Relatives caring for a severely dependent elderly person may experience all these feelings, together with the additional pressure from the perceived obligation to be loving and self-sacrificing since the elderly person is not a patient but a parent or close relative. Being depended upon provides the carer with the opportunity to demonstrate love, care and strength but it may also make both physical and psychological demands which are hard to meet. These are evident most clearly when care is for people who are severely dependent by virtue of gross mental and/or physical handicap but they are present in less extreme circumstances, such as the elderly person suffering from dementia who asks 'Where am I?' every five minutes. However much the caretaker understands that the elderly person really does not know because she cannot retain the information, it is still not easy to respond sensitively each time. It is important to remember that some very dependent elderly people require aspects of care which are appropriate for young children; we have come to accept that the dependence of young children arouses in their carers strong feelings of love but also of violence and that these are *normal*. This understanding should be given more readily to the carers for severely dependent adults, who may be frightened by the intensity of their reactions or by the rapidity with which concern and love may be followed by irritation and annoyance. But because of the nature of the subject, it may be necessary for the social worker to comment on the normality of these feelings and to ask outright about how the caretaker feels about the kind of care that is necessary for the elderly person. Not only might this offer the opening for a caretaker to admit to being rough or at times uncaring in attitude but it may reveal the equally important instances of overprotection.

The strength of ambivalent feelings that may be present in a close relationship is eloquently described in the following quotation from an account by a woman in her seventies who was caring for her elderly husband who had been disabled by a stroke (Wicke, 1978). It was her wish to have him home four days a week, with the local hospital providing care during the remaing three:

Sometimes it is *merciless* for patience breaks and weariness takes over,

> we are no longer young and time is running out ... The ups and downs we have encountered are innumerable – the sudden 'freezing' when walking, the awful loss of temper on both sides, the tears of sheer despair because he cannot express himself and constantly says 'yes' when he means 'no' ... The strain on my patience and his has been almost unendurable and yet it is still wonderful to have him home ...

For many elderly people and their caretakers, a period of severe dependency precedes death. This can be a period of particularly poignant and intimate feelings and it will not be easy for the dying person and the caretakers to face what is happening. The intensity of the experience of witnessing the dying of an elderly parent has been vividly described by de Beauvoir (1969) who recorded the 'pictures, nightmares and sadnesses' of being with her mother during the last thirty days of her mother's life. She then wrote (p. 82) of the benefits that she and her sister had gained from that painful experience:

> We did derive an undoubted good from [that time]; it saved us, or almost saved us, from remorse ... Since you never do all you might for anyone – not even within the arguable limits that you have set yourself – you have plenty of room left for reproach ... We felt that we atoned for [our omissions] by the days we gave up to her, by the peace of mind that our being there gave her and by the victories gained over fear and pain.

In certain circumstances the social worker may have a particularly important part in this terminal stage of life. Elderly people who are alone, for example, may need to talk about their impending death and the social worker might be the only person with whom this is possible. Or the staff in a residential home or geriatric ward might need special support, perhaps when several old people have died in a short space of time. The impact of death on the staff and the residents of homes has been little studied, yet it is not uncommon for staff to be caring for elderly residents at a time when their own parents are becoming increasingly frail. A third possible area for social work intervention is, of course, with the relatives or spouses who are providing care; it may be that with support they will be better able to cope, or that they need help to acknowledge that the burden is too great for them. Many of the carers for elderly people will themselves be old or faced with competing demands from their own families, but it will not be easy for them to face the limits of their own ability to provide direct care. However, it will not be possible for a social worker to become involved in such work unless he has resolved personal fears, conflicts and needs in relation to his own ageing and the ageing of his parents.

BEREAVEMENT, LOSS AND ISOLATION

Old people will normally experience a variety of losses, not all of which will be major and some of which may at least be found to have important compensatory factors. Some old people, however, will experience loss that is both multiple and accumulated, to an extent rarely experienced by people when they are young. The loss may be of spouse, siblings or close friends; of home; of physical function; and the loss of one may be followed by others, as when a woman who has had a stroke loses her caring husband and then has to move into residential care. The impact of these experiences, coming so quickly one upon the other, is yet to be fully understood. What are the coping mechanisms required to withstand successive onslaughts of this nature? And at a time when one is oneself becoming more frail?

Widowhood and major loss of function are often identified by old people as marking the beginning of a different, often unhappy phase in their life. The chronic, all-pervasive sadness as a part of widowhood is described by elderly people in successive studies (Tunstall, 1966; Townsend in Shanas *et al.*, 1968; Hadley *et al.*, 1975). The recently bereaved are particularly vulnerable to physical and mental ill-health (Isaacs and Neville, 1976; Goldberg and Neill, 1972; Arie, 1973).

There is some evidence to suggest that the pattern of grief may be slightly different in old people. Most studies of grief are of younger people (Marris, 1958; Parkes, 1972a) and the sequence of so-called 'typical' grief – initial shock and numbness, followed by acute distress and then by a longer period of sadness through to gradual reintegration – has been well documented. But this 'typical' grief may not be so common amongst elderly people and their manifestation of grief may, therefore, pass unnoticed, possibly also giving rise to the impression that their old age gives them an immunity to the pain.

Gramlich (1973) suggests that 'inhibited' or 'chronic' grief may be common amongst elderly people. The significance of inhibited grief is that, whilst appearing subdued, it is long-lasting and may well be associated with physical or psychological symptoms. Chronic grief, as its name suggests, is associated with intense feeling over a longer time-span than is found in typical grief and may also give rise to hostility, suspicion or apathy. Like inhibited grief, chronic grief may well present in the form of physical symptoms, frequently in the months immediately following bereavement but maybe for a period of up to two years after the death. Gramlich is writing for doctors presented with the overt physical symptoms of old people but the following point (p. 107) is equally relevant for social workers: 'Most elderly patients actually hurt rather than complain of emotional pain ... One should suspect a grief reaction, regardless of symptomatology, when one sees an individual who has sustained a major loss within the two years prior to the presenting complaints.'

Gramlich stresses the importance of encouraging old people (except those who are physically or mentally very frail) to express their grief and of helping them to recognise the significance of their bereavement as the precipitating factor in their present state of dis-ease. When the elderly person who is bereaved is living on his/her own and either has no immediate family or lives some distance away from them, there will be few opportunities to share memories of the dead spouse. Yet this is a vital part of healthy grief and, deprived of opportunities to express sadness, happiness and just the ordinary emotions, the bereaved person may become 'stuck' in his grief, unable to re-establish an equilibrium. It may also be that the memory of a bereavement many years ago is reawakened by this latest tragedy, as the following case example from a social worker illustrates:

> One woman had joined the [day care] group because she was depressed. Her husband had died recently and she'd had a fall – but in actual fact the root of her trouble was that she'd never got over the death of her daughter who died in the war aged sixteen. And we went all through the party dresses she'd made for her, the green silk dress she'd worn only once, the shoes that were dyed to match, how she'd had TB ... That woman is a changed character now, it's incredible.

The prevalence of unresolved grief has been noted in a study where physically frail elderly people have been offered intensive domiciliary services to enable them to remain in their own homes rather than enter an institution (Dunnachie, 1979). It would seem to be a factor of which social workers need to be particularly aware; how many referrals on elderly people come within two years of a bereavement, for example? Certainly it is not unusual for recent bereavement to precipitate a request for admission to residential care. The social worker may, however, have to take the lead in raising the subject of death and of bereavement. For many reasons, an elderly person may not think it appropriate to do so or may feel unable to unburden himself without first being shown that the worker regards this as permissible. This point is of relevance also for home helps who may well have the closest and most regular contact with an elderly person and, therefore, may be the most appropriate and perhaps the only persons with whom grief can be shared.

The emphasis so far has been on grief following the death of a loved one, but it is well established that grief may follow other significant forms of loss or change (Marris, 1974). Parkes (1972b) described the feelings expressed by a group of young widows and by a group of young amputees; he then compared these with the reactions of a group of young women rehoused following a slum-clearance project. There is a remarkable similarity in the words used by all three groups to explain their feelings: 'mutilation', 'emptiness' and 'painful loss' constantly occur and symptoms of grief were reported irrespective of the nature of the loss experienced. Even the young women who had been pleased at the prospect of a better standard of housing and who appreciated their improved dwellings reported that they nevertheless also experienced a sense of loss which was at times severe. It would be instructive to explore in similar fashion the response of elderly people to admission to residential care or to disability following a stroke or amputation.

Whilst many elderly people display an, at times, remarkable resilience – as indeed do other sections of the population faced with major and perhaps long-term stress – there is a proportion who may be said to be partially or even totally defeated in their attempt to preserve some dignity and integrity of self. Tunstall (1966) estimated that just over 6 per cent of his national survey came within this category; Hadley *et al.* (1975) found 29 per cent of their sample could be described as living in circumstances which were 'miserable and pathetic' (the fact that there was a preponderance of people aged 80 and over in this sample may at least partly explain the discrepancy between the two sets of figures).

Such elderly people can be seen as living in a state of isolation and deprivation, without the comfort or the company of others, with little involvement in the world about them, and with few opportunities for choice, even of the most basic and elementary kind. Hadley *et al.* noted (p. 40) that they seemed 'dominated' by feelings of loneliness:

> When the interviewer started asking questions on loneliness, the old people often broke down and cried. Their replies frequently suggested confusion and fear of the future, and sometimes seemed to indicate a diminution of their sense of identity ... 'Sometimes I can't sort of face myself. I can't see how it will all end up.'

This feeling that one's self and one's environment are in a state of disintegration has been identified as one of the possible consequences of profound or multiple loss. The value and purpose of life may be doubted; Erikson (1979), writing about the survivors of an American town destroyed when a dam burst, described the inability to think of the future and the sense of futility exhibited by those who had witnessed and suffered from the tragedy. The incidence of suicide within the elderly population raises questions as to how far this is a consequence of a life that has become desolate or without purpose.

Studies suggest that perhaps as many as 30 per cent of all known suicides are by elderly people; amongst those who kill themselves there is a high incidence of recent bereavement and/or severe disability and social isolation. Whereas young people may attempt suicide but are prevented from succeeding because they are discovered in time or because the method was not lethal, old people often have both the means (medication) and the living circumstances (isolation) to make sure they succeed (Shulman, 1978). Moreover, although suicidal thoughts may not be openly acknowledged, the risk of suicide may be evident in the extent to which an old person sees his life as empty and purposeless.

When elderly people are living in such emotional and social

deprivation, an important task for the social worker is in attempting to maintain or preserve the client's sense of identity as an individual and as a member of society. The way in which this may be achieved may involve deceptively simple activities which are nevertheless about the elementary discussions and choices that are part of most people's everyday lives. Thus enabling a disabled or isolated person to go to a clothes shop or making use of pictures in mail order catalogues offers the opportunity to choose colour and style; through such an activity, the client has the opportunity to engage in a number of related tasks which involve decision-making and relating to other people and which act as a stimulus to self-expression. In residential or day care settings, choice of food may be one of the major areas of choice still open to people whose circumstances have been restricted through infirmity; the following is an account by a social worker organising a group to provide day care:

> It's self-determination on a very basic level – like do you want brown bread or white, chocolate biscuit or ginger snap. If for a long time they have not been given that opportunity to choose, then they talk about it and appreciate it ... And with the ones who are socially isolated, it's surprising how quickly they come back into it all ... Even 90 year olds can make new relationships, I've watched it happen. You see the improvement, the happiness. You see somebody who was cowed and white and very insecure get a better skin colour, be more assured and able to joke and laugh ... And you see them begin to help each other, you look across the room and hear a conversation and see smiles and hear the laughs.

Two points need emphasising here. The first is that work with clients who have become socially and emotionally deprived is much concerned with the *restoration* of those aspects of daily life which the less deprived can confidently take for granted. It is often forgotten that choosing clothes, food, and so on involves us in a wide range of activities – decision-making, self-expression, relationships with others, use of money – and these are fundamental to being a person in society. (The therapeutic value of the apparently routine nature of daily living tasks has been explored by Gunzburg and Gunzburg, 1973, in relation to working with mentally handicapped people and is equally relevant for work with some elderly people.)

The second point to emphasise is that the apparently simple nature of the help being offered should not obscure the sensitivity and the skill required of the worker who may be faced by a client whose apathy or sense of hopelessness is a major obstacle to the introduction of any kind of change. Accepting the client's perception of his situation, working with his low self-esteem, offering encouragement and the prospect of improvement without forcing him to accept help or over-riding a genuine wish to be alone – all this requires considerable knowledge, skill and perseverance.

MENTAL IMPAIRMENT

This fourth and final section on the problems that may confront elderly people focuses on the care of those who are suffering from dementia – an irreversible and often also progressive degeneration of the brain. It is estimated that the total number of elderly people suffering from dementia in 1977 was 715,000; by the turn of the century, the number may have risen to 727,000 (Office of Health Economics, 1979). About one in ten people aged 65 and over and living in the community suffers from moderate or severe dementia and the incidence increases markedly in the very old: about one in five of those aged 80 and over and living in the community will be affected.

It is important that these figures are put into some perspective. On the one hand, in terms of our understanding of ageing, we should not lose sight of the fact that although one in five people over 80 will suffer to some degree, the other lesson to be drawn from that information is that four out of five will not. 'Going senile' is not therefore the norm, even amongst the very old. On the other hand, there is no doubt that when an elderly person becomes demented, the burden of care to be borne by families, neighbours and community services is usually great. Some six out of every seven people with dementia live in the community and although some will not be severely affected, others will require a good deal of care and supervision of a kind that is difficult to organise and often stressful to provide. Dementia is the 'prime determinant' (Arie, 1977) of breakdown in family or community care and elderly people with dementia are major users of both long- and short-term hospital and residential care.

Dementia is but one of the psychiatric disorders found in the elderly population; the epidemiological studies carried out in Newcastle found that neurotic or character disorders were present in 12 per cent of elderly people and a major functional psychosis in about 2 per cent (Kay *et al.*, 1964). Many of these disorders can be successfully treated or at least considerably controlled. The prognosis for someone with dementia is not so hopeful: there is no cure for the disorder, it is often progressive and it is significantly associated with a diminution in life expectancy (although even so, this may be measured in terms of a couple of years rather than in months). Environment, a sensitive approach by the caretakers and careful use of medication to control some symptoms, for example, the extreme restlessness or agitation that may be present, can make an important difference to the behaviour of the demented person but this cannot obscure the fact that dementia is irreversible and likely to lead to a general decline in mental and possibly also physical capacities.

A major difficulty for those concerned with the care of elderly people is that the clinical manifestations of dementia are not unique to that disorder. Depression may present in a form similar to dementia. Impairment of memory, disorientation in time and place and wandering may follow bereavement or a move to a new environment; confused behaviour may also be the result of an acute urinary or respiratory infection, of certain deficiency states or of the action of medication prescribed for other illnesses. Accurate and early diagnosis is therefore vital since these confusional states usually disappear if the underlying pathology is treated. The consequences of doing nothing because 'it's just old age' can result in permanent damage to the elderly person and a precipitate diagnosis of dementia can demonstrate all the unwelcome consequences of labelling which have been noted in the past in relation to schizophrenia or psychopathy. Yet elderly people suffering from dementia may be unknown to their general practitioner and the presence of dementia may be overlooked by the doctor even when he is in contact with an elderly patient for some other reason. The evidence of a study by Williamson *et al.* (1964) showed that 80 per cent of old people with moderate or severe dementia who were living at home were not known by their doctor to be demented. Isaacs and Neville (1976), in their somewhat smaller study, also found that psychiatric disorders in general and dementia in particular had often not been diagnosed by general practitioners. That same study found, as have others, that the elderly patients of general practitioners are considerably less likely than patients from other age-groups to be referred for investigative treatment or specialist consultation. Whilst this may in part be a consequence of the generally low expectations of health amongst elderly people, it also reflects the level of knowledge about geriatrics and the attitudes towards the illnesses of old people that are to be found amongst general practitioners.

Most social workers will become involved with demented elderly people not at this initial diagnostic stage but when problems of management or 'disposal' arise because the person's memory has become so impaired that he constitutes a fire risk or his disoriented behaviour imposes an intolerable burden on neighbours or family. Typically the request that 'something should be done' comes in connection with an identified problem or problems of which the elderly person is unaware and by which he is untroubled. He is therefore an involuntary client who is not motivated to receive help and who may indeed be suspicious of outsiders. Justification for intervention and for determining the limits of that intervention are not easy to define, especially since the needs of the client and others around him may be in conflict.

A useful article by Wasser (1971) considers the nature of social work with mentally impaired elderly people. Wasser emphasises the importance of responding to the need rather than to the wishes of elderly people who are unable to articulate or even to recognise when they require help (p. 576): 'the worker does not wait to be asked, but ... introduces what is needed, assuming agreement unless there is marked rejection. The worker presumes that the client develops a taste for service by tasting it.'

This approach is somewhat different from the customary one in which the client's involvement in and co-operation with the activities of the social worker are an essential part of intervention. With the provision of 'protective services', as Wasser describes them, the principle of client self-determination has to be practised in a manner which acknowledges the client's limited capacity for decision-making and self-care but which preserves those areas of decision-making of which he is still capable. This is at times a difficult task for the social worker and there are no easy means of resolving the tensions inherent in a situation where an elderly person is apparently content with a way of life which is potentially dangerous to himself or to others. However, the existence of the tension is one of the important safeguards for the client, since it should act as a check on precipitate or excessive interference by the professional in the life of an individual whose behaviour may be seen as flouting the norms of society.

A further difficulty in working with elderly people suffering from dementia is that their experience of themselves and of their world does not accord with the reality of others. Precisely what they are experiencing may not be easy to ascertain and the logic of their actions may evade the onlooker; the world of someone with dementia is often very private and individual. One clue to the meaning of what is going on may lie in an understanding of the demented person's earlier life; certain patterns of seemingly bizarre behaviour may make sense in the context of past employment or past family relationships. The start of an interesting project was reported in the journal *Mind Out* (no. 30, p. 9) whereby audio-visual reminders of the Second World War (ration books, photographs, the sound of air raid warning sirens, films, and so on) were being used to see if these 'reminiscence aids' would facilitate meaningful contact between some quite severely demented elderly patients and their nurses.

If the behaviour and thought patterns of the demented person sometimes have little meaning to the onlooker, the same may often apply the other way around. Sudden or abrupt movements may be interpreted as hostile or alarming; the use of cot sides to the bed may appear sinister rather than protective. The ease with which actions and perceptions can be misinterpreted has been well illustrated in some accounts of the experience of mental illness: the reflection of the window frame on the bedroom wall which appears like prison bars is an understandable misrepresentation of one's surroundings. It is perhaps no coincidence that elderly people may become more disoriented at night (as indeed may children who have been removed from their customary environment). This is the time when, for all of us, perception is less reliable and shadowy outlines are capable of several interpretations.

Through the use of certain techniques it may be possible to encourage a moderately confused elderly person to establish former links with reality. At a simple level, the use of large clocks and calendars in hospital wards or residential homes provides evidence of time; given that the sight of many old people is failing, they may have real difficulty in seeing the ordinary-size clock high up on the wall at one end of the room or in reading the date on a newspaper. Reality orientation is one method, based on reception and relearning, which aims to re-establish some links with the present by providing the old person with regular and consistent information about who the staff are, where he is and who he is, and so on (Weiner *et al.*, 1978). Consistency of approach is important; too often the confused person may be fobbed off with quick answers to his questions and each caretaking person may answer differently. To take one example: the elderly person who says insistently 'I am going home now' may be met with a variety of obstacles to his plan as he moves from one staff member to another and each gives his own reason why going home is not possible – because the buses are not running, because it is bed-time/lunch-time or because the old person has to see the doctor first. Or promises are given that the old person can go home 'tomorrow'. If an old person is known to have certain fixed questions or statements, the response should be honest and the same from all those in a caring role or else it feeds into the confusion. If something is always promised for tomorrow and tomorrow never comes, how does that help someone who is disoriented in time?

This section has been intended to highlight a few points that are especially relevant for work with old people suffering from dementia. This is not to imply that social work with such clients forms a discrete body of skills or knowledge. Much that appertains to work with demented clients – means of communication, the help to be offered to families who are involved in caring, or the management of risk – also has a wider application and for that reason has been discussed elsewhere rather than restricted to the one problem area.

Chapter 3

Some Aspects of Direct Work

In Chapter 1 it was suggested that social workers may have deep-seated, but possibly unrecognised, fears and prejudices about old age and that these inhibit involvement with the problems presented by people who are old. It has been recognised in respect of other clients – notably those who are mentally ill – that social workers do not necessarily begin with a 'neutral' attitude towards certain aspects of their work. Mental illness still retains some of its capacity to evoke fear and suspicion and a part of the supervision of students and practitioners who are learning about work with mentally ill people will be an exploration of attitudes towards mental illness and psychiatric hospitals. It may be argued that similar consideration of old age is necessary if social work skills with elderly people are to be developed.

However, alongside the negative attitudes towards old age, and possibly also contributing to them, there exists an uncertainty about how to engage in direct work with elderly clients. This is no doubt part of what Rapoport *et al.* (1975, p. 319) have described as 'a large area of cultural inadequacy in general techniques for relating to old people' and it is expressed in comments such as the following, both from qualified and experienced social workers in an area team who had had little contact with elderly clients:

> I tend to be more 'resources and procedures conscious' with the elderly because I don't feel I know enough to consider methods of intervention, goals, etc., in relation to these clients.

and:

> The difficulty is treatment. There isn't the theoretical framework for treatment as there is for family work. Whoever heard of behaviour modification with the elderly? Social workers' casework eggs are all in a different basket from the elderly.

Both these comments suggest that there may be something of a professional vacuum so far as practice with elderly clients is concerned. Part of this may be due to a confusion or a lack of understanding about the potential for change and achievement by old people. This is examined in this chapter in the first section on pace and goals. The second section describes a case example of communication; and the third, on the use of reminiscence, demonstrates that it is important for social workers to be alert to the meaning of memories and the purpose that is served by an elderly person's accounts of past events and experiences. Without an understanding of what is happening in an interview, the social worker may miss opportunities for meaningful contact with his client.

CHANGE, GOALS AND THE PACE OF WORK

An aspect of old age that is often forgotten or underestimated is that it is a period of life in which many changes, on several dimensions, take place. Eisdorfer (1977, p. 60) suggests that 'analogies between the aged and adolescent periods of life, so far as accelerated physical, environmental and social change rates are involved, are valid to contemplate' and, amongst others, de Beauvoir (1977) also emphasises the energy that is involved in ageing. She describes being old as (p. 540) 'a very moving struggle' to retain identity, integrity and purpose in the face of economic and social deprivation. (It is important to remember that both Eisdorfer and de Beauvoir are talking about the process of *normal* ageing and not the circumstances that follow disability caused by trauma or the onset of mental infirmity.) The fact that so many old people cope with ageing without need of outside help is a significant indicator of their capacity to adjust to change in themselves and in the world around them.

Elderly people who need social work help are likely to be those for whom the struggle has become or is becoming too much. It is salutary to reflect on the circumstances that may bring elderly people to the attention of health and welfare services and to consider the kind of decisions they are sometimes asked to make. Should they move to their daughter's, to sheltered accommodation, or to residential care? Should they have what might be a major operation? Can they afford, in all senses of the word, to take a risk or can they afford not to? Will they be able to manage even though their sight or hearing is beginning to fail?

Bearing in mind the kind of adjustments required of elderly people and the variety of changes inflicted upon them, it is remarkable that the adjective 'challenging' seems to occur so seldom in descriptions of direct work with elderly clients. Indeed, as has been mentioned earlier, it is more likely that the emphasis will be on constraints: goals should be 'modest' and the pace of work will be 'slow'. Both these commonly held views of social work with elderly people are open to question on a number of counts.

To begin with, they are generalisations and as such suffer from a lack of attention to individual circumstances. Social work goals cannot be meaningfully considered without reference to the context of the client, the worker, or the resources available. This point can be illustrated with reference to the apparently straightforward and easy goal of arranging a home help for a disabled elderly client. The client may have devoted her life to the role of housewife, so that the prospect of an outsider coming in to take over certain aspects of this role represents a threat to identity. On the other hand, the client may be willing to accept the service, but domiciliary resources may be under severe pressure. In both instances the goal of providing a home help becomes anything but modest and considerable skill will be required of the social worker either in direct work with the client or in putting a forceful argument to the home help organiser or more senior member of staff.

Perlman (1957, p. 201) writes of the need to balance 'desirable goals ... against feasible ones' and she warns of the frustrations that follow when goals (p. 199) 'are conceived as complete resolution of problems, including those of personality'. This emphasis on 'feasible' goals has become an increasingly important part of social work practice as social work has become more concerned with defining areas of effectiveness. It is recognised that major changes in attitude, behaviour and feeling are 'notoriously difficult to achieve' (Vickery, 1977, p. 29) for almost all clients and those who are elderly are no exception. Moreover, it must be remembered that the problems of some elderly people are the problems of a lifetime; they may have always been inclined to be a bit 'difficult', 'touchy', depressed, or anxious and in their old age they have retained these characteristics. The likelihood of being able to find 'solutions' so long after such behaviour or attitudes first became established is slim indeed.

Other elderly clients, however, are faced with the need to adapt to changes that have been inflicted upon them: disability or bereavement, for example. A major adjustment is required by those who enter residential care. Goldberg *et al*. (1970) noted the increasing difficulty experienced by elderly clients who faced successive and accumulated changes – a consequence not necessarily of frailty due to ageing but of the immobilising and overwhelming effect of multiple change. In the face of this, it may be important for social worker and client to select one or two discrete areas for intervention.

The developments in practice from Perlman to the task-centred approach of Reid and Epstein (1972) have demonstrated the value of partialising the problems to be tackled and aiming at those which client and worker have the best chance of solving or ameliorating. Cormican (1977) has described the appropriateness of a task-centred approach to the problems of many elderly clients (an example is given in Chapter 5 in the discussion of the management of risk). She noted that through participating in the identification of goals, taking responsibility for certain parts of the task to be achieved and seeing a successful result in a short space of time, an elderly person is made aware of strengths and an ability to succeed which have survived the losses he may have experienced. Achievement is not often part of some elderly people's lives and it may provide a valuable corrective if much of their life has become associated with weaknesses. Furthermore, success may have an important 'ripple' effect: improving morale and increasing confidence at tackling other problems. The benefits of short-term work with elderly clients have been little explored; the stereotype is that long-term involvement is always necessary. (It is true that elderly clients referred to a social services department may form the majority who become 'long term', Goldberg *et al*., 1978, but it is important to note that in the main, they do not receive on-going, regular social work help but occasional review or surveillance visits. This is of a different order from the understanding of 'long-term work' as it applies to children in care or community support for a mentally ill person and it is questionable whether such episodic contact is always an appropriate task for social workers.)

One can only speculate on the influence of social workers' expectations upon the way in which their work with a client develops. There is evidence that in respect of much of their work, many social workers frequently do not have a clearly defined goal, plan of action or an understanding of what might constitute a reason for withdrawing and this no doubt contributes to some cases remaining 'open' for longer than necessary. (Goldberg and Fruin, 1976). Work with elderly clients therefore must be placed in the context of a pattern of work which is often not clearly conceptualised. However, there are additional factors that may affect the nature of the social worker's intervention with elderly clients.

In certain instances, the social worker will be faced by obvious constraints, such as the client's limited capacity to speak, to retain information or to cope with more than a short interview. Preoccupation with anxieties about personal security may also influence a client's speed of thought and movement: unexpected falls or spells of dizziness are strong reasons for proceeding with caution. Loneliness and limited opportunities to discuss difficulties or even to exchange conversation may also make the client unwilling to allow the interview to end. It was noted earlier that the extent of the losses suffered by some elderly people takes time to absorb and to cope with; the decisions that may have to be made are not easy, as an officer-in-charge pointed out: 'When people have problems and are in a state of anxiety of any kind, they find it very difficult to give you answers and it doesn't matter how old they are.'

For these reasons, work with some elderly people has been found to take time and patience and the pace of work both within interviews and overall has been influenced by the need for some clients to proceed slowly and carefully. But there is a danger that, because he expects slowness, the social worker will find it; he may assume a somewhat passive role, albeit unknowingly, and allow interviews to drift or to become repetitive and routine without an identified purpose. The same officer-in-charge had this to say on the subject of the pace of work: 'If your idea is that once someone is over 75, it's goodbye, then the work is not only slow – it's dead.'

Alternatively, the social worker may misunderstand the reason for the client's difficulty in comprehension or reply, because this conforms to the stereotype of problems with concentration and inability to conduct a sensible conversation which are thought typical of the ageing process. Slight deafness or loss of visual acuity, both of which might be remediable, therefore pass unnoticed and remain uncorrected. Undetected deafness is estimated to be particularly common amongst old people, including those who are resident in elderly persons' homes (Martin and Peckford, 1978).

Thus, as with any client, the social worker should not make assumptions about his role in advance of seeing the client; nor should he impose his own expectations on the course of the interviews. The principle of the individuality of each client is an essential part of social work practice and it is this which should lead social workers to explore and question the nature and purpose of their work with each elderly client. It is to be noted that Biestek (1961, p. 29) states that assessment of the appropriate pace of work with each client 'is the guide and test' of individualisation which is his first principle of casework. Wider application of this principle in relation to elderly clients would be to their advantage.

COMMUNICATION – A CASE EXAMPLE

Elderly clients who are alone and without close relationships may have few opportunities to experience physical contact with other people and the social worker's ability to use touch unselfconsciously may be an important means of conveying caring. In the following account a social worker is describing how the combination of words and touch was an important feature of one day's work with a client who was in the admission ward of a geriatric unit.

During the course of the morning's ward round the doctor had seen a patient (Mrs Randall) and decided she would have to be moved to a long-term ward. He had not actually said as much to her and the decision had been made quite rapidly but almost certainly in her hearing. The social worker had not been involved in the discussion but knew of its content and was aware that although the long-term wards were never referred to as such, patients transferred from the admission ward fully realised the significance of the move. She had little opportunity during the ward round to talk to Mrs Randall and essentially, as she described later: 'I just stood there, longer than I might have done, just holding her hand,' adding: 'I do wish the doctor wouldn't ignore patients when he can't do anything more for them.' Later that day, when the social worker was back in the ward, Mrs Randall had called her over and:

> She got hold of my hand and started to cry, saying, 'They're moving me ... I've been knowing it would come and then today the doctor didn't say good morning to me so I knew the time had come. They're moving me – well, at least I'll stop there till I die, shan't I?'

The social worker continued:

> I said, 'Yes, I know they're moving you, but you know we don't have an alternative, don't you, these wards are not for people who need a lot of care' ... And when she said about being there till she died, I didn't say it to her but it looks like it to me, too, though a change of environment has been known to work wonders and physically, she could walk, she's just given up. And so I said, 'Well, it doesn't always follow, I know this is what it looks like now, but if perhaps you could get yourself walking again ...' And I suppose I spent about an hour talking about the new ward and why she had to go there and just holding her ...

and it seemed that eventually some of Mrs Randall's distress and apprehension had diminished. When the social worker left, Mrs Randall had apparently been able to talk about the move with fewer expressions of despair and hopelessness – 'Oh, I shall be all right' she had said with some determination.

Several points emerge from this example. First, and perhaps most important, is the fact that avoiding contact with someone, as the doctor did, can, paradoxically, be an eloquent form of communication. Secondly, Mrs Randall's awareness is a reminder that the client's capacity for understanding what is happening should never be underestimated; the social worker is faced by the need to respond as honestly and directly as Mrs Randall did, yet without destroying her. Mrs Randall's comment 'Well at least I'll stop there till I die, shan't I?' is capable of several interpretations: anger; an honest but sad recognition of the future; perhaps some relief at the end of uncertainty about what will happen to her; perhaps also a search for reassurance that she *will* get better. It is possible that she is saying all these things, at different levels but at the same time, in a manner not dissimilar to the mixture of vain hope, honest appraisal and denial that can be expressed by people who know they are terminally ill (Kübler-Ross, 1969).

Thirdly, this example shows that touch was welcomed, indeed initiated, by the client and perhaps enabled her to discuss such a painful subject more freely. The use of touch with young children or by nurses when adult patients are in pain is an accepted means of conveying a range of caring and protective feelings, as well as simply acknowledging and sharing another person's pain or distress. Elderly people who are recently bereaved may also benefit from such contact, especially if there is no close friend or relative who can offer the comfort so desperately needed. It is unfortunate that the rules and taboos that control the use of touch may inhibit social workers – especially those in the field setting where, unlike in the residential setting, the opportunities to communicate through physical contact are less likely to arise in uncontrived circumstances.

REMINISCENCE

The final part of this chapter considers the importance of the social worker's understanding and subsequent use of the memories and reminiscences which often form a major part of the conversation of elderly people. An elderly person's interest in the past may be explained by perceptual abilities, memory and his motivation for engaging in the present. Increasing sensory deficits may make for difficulty in the ability to learn new behaviour and to adapt to the conditions of a changing society. Social isolation may limit the old person's opportunity to explore and master the present. For some old people, the past will be a preferable alternative to the present, again perhaps because he is for some reason cut off from family or social contacts or because he is unable to accept his old age.

Alternatively, reminiscence can be used as an effective defence against discussion of the past or the future. A social worker described her unsuccessful attempts to encourage a client to consider arrangements for her discharge home now that her recovery from a minor fall had been complete:

> Mrs James now – I spent ages with her last week. But she won't let you get a word in. I feel that if only I could talk to her and get her to talk about what it's meant to her to have a fall – I feel I could help her if I could get to the core, but she won't let you. I'm afraid I got impatient with her – perhaps I haven't handled her in the right way. You get these feelings, don't you, that perhaps you're not doing everything you could, but ...

In the end, the doctor told Mrs James bluntly that it was either discharge or transfer to another ward, and at this point she agreed to consider the kind of help she would need in order to return to her home. The social worker expressed some unease at what she thought might seem 'rather brutal' treatment of Mrs James, yet it was clear that it took the combination of the authority of the doctor and his refusal to collude with Mrs James to bring her to the point of facing the present.

The readiness of so many elderly clients to share their past is, for many workers, one of the enjoyable aspects of work with this age-group. In describing her work with an elderly man whose slow recovery from illness was causing understandable depression, a social worker described how she valued the opportunity to learn more about recent social and economic history:

> One enjoyment of working with the elderly is that some of them have had very interesting lives and if they are prepared to talk about their lives, it's amazing what you learn. I have recently had an old gentleman aged 94, who writes poetry. He is very interesting talking about things ninety years ago.

The importance of memories in establishing and reinforcing identity has been recognised in work with children in care who may lose touch with the significant people and events in their lives. Tizard (1977) quotes an example of a child, placed for adoption at an age when she had memories of previous caretakers, who was helped to understand her past by her adoptive mother who sought photographs, letters, and so on, which were placed in a scrapbook. In this way child and parent explored the reasons (pp. 143–4) 'why she is brown with curly hair, how she came to live in a children's home and why she is one of the "adopted" children in our family'.

Butler (1974) emphasised that reminiscence (or the 'life review') is an important part of the process of successful ageing. He draws attention to the uniqueness of reminiscence in old age as opposed to at any other time of life (p. 534): 'only in old age can one experience a personal sense of the entire life cycle'. He explains the purpose of the life review thus:

> the life review is characterised by a progressive return to consciousness of past experience, in particular the resurgence of unresolved conflicts which can now be surveyed and integrated. The old are not only taking stock of themselves as they review their past lives; they are trying to think and feel through what they will do with the time that is left and whatever material and emotional legacies they may have to give to others ... If unresolved conflicts and fears are successfully reintegrated they can give new significance and meaning to an individual's life in preparing for death and mitigating fears.

It is interesting that Butler's interpretation adds weight to Eisdorfer's suggested analogy of old age with adolescence that was quoted earlier in this chapter. Adolescence, as a developmental phase, is also one in which past experiences may be reappraised, unresolved conflicts worked through and a sense of personal identity established.

Several writers on social work with elderly people have described how the worker can use reminiscence to help elderly clients resolve some of their present emotional or interpersonal difficulties (Wasser, 1966; Pincus, 1970; Cormican, 1977). The following two case examples illustrate this. In the first, a social worker was talking about an elderly woman whom she had admitted to residential care. Throughout her life, this woman had worked a small-holding and orchard and her decision to enter care was her reluctant acknowledgement that she could no longer continue her life as an active countrywoman. Her conversations with her social worker were full of her memories of the vegetables and fruit she had harvested so successfully over the years and of her gardening skills, now apparently useless, and the social worker came to realise that these memories were serving to point up the contrast between the independence then and the dependence now. Thus the worker focused on encouraging her client to apply her experiences of the past to the garden and grounds of the old people's home and in doing so was able to help her client transfer the value and usefulness of an important part of her life to her present circumstances. (In passing, the worker pointed out how important it had been to enlist the co-operation of the gardener so that he did not become angry when offered advice as to when and where to plant the flowers.)

In a second example, another social worker described her work with an old man, admitted to hospital seriously ill. He did not talk about his present situation but dwelt on his experiences in the First World War – life in the trenches, the suffering and the deaths he had witnessed. The social worker thought that through these descriptions of other people's deaths then, the man was talking about his own imminent death, and about the meaning of life and that, in addition, he was working through the horrors of that time which had remained with him ever since. But, as the social worker said, much depended on what was heard 'behind' the words, through the tone of his voice and through the expression of thoughts which were focused on events of sixty years ago but were not specific to that time.

In both these situations, the social worker had made an assessment of what the reminiscence meant to the client. The second example in particular is one which illustrates what Cormican (1977, p. 491) has termed *functional reminiscing*, where a client is able to come to terms with an aspect of his past and to achieve an acceptance of the present. The social worker requires skill in facilitating this process; in the course of an interview it will be necessary to make decisions about when to encourage and when to discourage further detail and how to direct and respond to the reminiscences in such a way that painful memories do not become overwhelming. Just as some depressed clients may dwell on the 'bad' parts of themselves, almost to the point of indulgence, so the reminiscences of an elderly client may focus on the unfulfilled parts of his life. The worker may therefore have an important role in redressing the balance, as it were, by reminding the client of good experiences and pointing to achievements which he has either forgotten or ignored. Goldberg *et al*. (1970, p. 198) observed from their study that it was possible in interviews to move from the distressing to the reassuring: 'Expression of feelings about painful situations often turned into reassuring and emotionally satisfying reminiscences which can help the old person to regain a sense of positive worth and identity.'

The response to a client's memories and the purposeful use of reminiscence as part of social work with elderly clients is, therefore, an aspect of practice which requires careful attention. Misjudgement of the significance of reminiscence may result in a failure to get to the cause of the problem; more seriously, it may leave the client less able to cope with the strength of his memories.

Chapter 4

Assessment for Social Service and for Social Work

Assessment is often considered in relation to particular resources, such as assessment of the need for residential care. In this chapter a different approach is adopted in that the focus is on several aspects of assessment as a task routinely undertaken by staff in social services departments. The organisational response to referrals on elderly people and the assessments that follow raise a number of important issues. Some of these are common to other client groups, for example, consideration of how practice should be influenced by knowledge of the client group concerned and of the theory and ethics of social work. Other points, whilst not unique to referrals on elderly people, have a particular relevance. An example here is the part played by non-social work staff (notably home help organisers and occupational therapists) or the relationship between social work and another profession such as health visiting.

There are two underlying themes to this chapter. The first is whether it is possible, desirable and useful to devise a schedule of questions which could form the 'core' of assessment interviews with clients who were previously unknown to the social services department; these questions could be asked irrespective of the nature of the referral or of the worker undertaking the interview (and providing, of course, the client agreed). Such an approach would have the advantage of ensuring that there is some uniformity of assessment procedures and this may be important for a client group which is known to be likely to put up with difficulties.

The second, and related theme is that identification of the more obvious practical needs should also provide reliable information as to the presence or otherwise of additional emotional or relationship problems for which social work help may be appropriate. Not every client will require or want social work support and certainly the provision of social service should not be dependent upon a social work recommendation. Nor is it feasible or even desirable that every client referred for social service also receives a separate assessment to see if social work help is appropriate. It is, however, important that elderly clients have *access* to social work help and if such access is to be offered before crises and emergencies make the presence of need obvious, then it is relevant to consider the role of social service staff in identification of what might be called the 'early warning signs' of likely future difficulties.

ASSESSMENT OF NEED

A fundamental part of assessment is the definition and recognition of need, by both client and worker. This is a complex subject, in which personal and professional values, experience, aspirations and understanding play a significant part, and here it is possible only to isolate some of the information that is most relevant to work with elderly people.

The assessment of need in the elderly population is carried out in the context of a low level of demand for service by the clients, or potential clients, themselves. This has major implications for staff undertaking assessment interviews in that the absence of demand by the client cannot be reliably ascribed to absence of need. At times, therefore, need is being defined by professionals according to standards which differ from those of the client; but on other occasions, professionals will be involved in encouraging clients to voice the need of which they are aware but for which, for whatever reason, they have not sought a remedy.

Crosbie (in Butcher and Crosbie, 1977) offers a useful description of the process by which an individual comes to identify need and then perhaps to express that need in the form of a request for a service. Crosbie suggests that there are four stages in the expression of need: first, the perception of dis-ease; secondly, an assessment that something should be done; thirdly, the knowledge that something *can* be done; and finally, the actual decision to take some action. At each stage, a person may 'opt out' from the process – not recognising that something is wrong, for example; believing (possibly incorrectly) that no help is possible or available; or finding the effort or the stigma of seeking help a disincentive to the expression of need.

The most striking examples of unrecognised or unreported need amongst elderly people are found in relation to their health, especially if the elderly person is very old or lives alone or with an elderly spouse. It was mentioned in a previous chapter that elderly people may accept discomfort as a normal part of ageing for which they believe no cure or relief is possible; their expectation of health is low and they therefore accept the 'minor miseries' such as painful feet, slight giddiness, constipation, or poor sleep and they approach the doctor only for more pronounced symptoms of ill-health (Williamson *et al.*, 1964; Goldberg *et al.*, 1970). Whatever the reasons for this (such as fear of painful treatment, a dread of admission to hospital, or a concern, shown by the population as a whole, not to 'bother' the doctor unless absolutely necessary) it is a cause for some concern since minor conditions, left untreated, may worsen or have far-reaching effects on later function – the possible consequences of not receiving adequate foot care being perhaps the simplest example of this. Yet, and this is equally important, this failure to report ill-health exists alongside a high regard for good health; elderly people in the studies by Hunt (1978) and Abrams (1978a) identified good health as either the first or the second condition of a satisfying old age.

A final point on the articulation of need is that people may decide, for whatever reason, to seek their own solution to the problem as they see it and here their understanding and knowledge about that problem is likely to influence the kind of solution they adopt. Butcher and Crosbie (1977) give a very good example of how an apparently minor, but potentially serious condition may be misinterpreted and possibly inappropriately 'solved'. They asked their elderly respondents what advice they would give a friend who felt tired all the time and had difficulty in shopping. Most of the answers offered practical suggestions such as applying for a home help to do the shopping or asking the local shop to deliver the goods. The researchers commented (pp. 100–1):

> few people (10%) actually mentioned the doctor as a relevant person to turn to ... Almost one in four respondents felt that the problem

> was, generally, one of growing old ... Thus in response to a very common problem which could have a medical cause, the majority of the sample said they would try a non-medical person first, then apply to the doctor, although a few ... would only turn to the GP as a very last resort ...

Perhaps this offers one explanation why the onset of diabetes or anaemia may remain undetected amongst elderly people, yet both are known to be not uncommon disorders in old age.

An interesting study by Chapman (1979) on the use of social services by elderly people draws attention not just to the incidence of unmet need for home help and meals-on-wheels in the total elderly population in a south London ward (11·2 and 2·2 per cent respectively) but also to the discrepancy between the figure of those who said they wanted help, and were thus referred, and those who then later received a service. For example (p. 65), of the 3·3 per cent who said they would like help with light housework, only 0·9 per cent eventually received a service. This cannot be totally explained by a shortage of supply – although it is worth noting that one survey estimated that the home help service needed to be increased by 20 per cent if it were fully to meet the needs of users (Hunt, 1970). Factors such as the client's determination to manage and the quality of the service offered are likely to influence eventual take-up as, of course, will the skill and perseverance of the interviewer in making help available in a way which does not threaten the client's self-respect.

ASSESSMENT – BY WHOM AND FOR WHAT?

Referrals on elderly people may constitute something in the region of 30 per cent of the intake to an area office (Goldberg *et al.*, 1978). They are unlikely to be self-referrals (self-referral is found mostly amongst clients with young children) and the majority will originate from staff in hospitals or in primary health care teams. Referrals often come in the form of a request for a specific service or resource and this is an important point since the service requested is likely to influence the disposal or allocation of the referral; requests for home help, for example, will in most departments be passed direct to the home help organiser to investigate and assessments for aids and adaptations to an occupational therapist (OT). The determinant of whether a social worker takes the referral may well be whether the assessment is for a resource, such as a place in a day centre or in residential care, which requires the application to be investigated by social work staff. Thus a number of social work and social service staff, with differing experience, knowledge and training, are engaged in assessing referrals that concern elderly people. To what extent should they cover similar ground in their interviews, differing only when they focus on their particular area of expertise? To what extent should they be concerned with the identification of need beyond that presented on the referral form? How broadly should they define the scope and content of their assessment interviews?

Questions such as these are not dissimilar to those to be asked of the role of the duty officer in social services departments. Indeed, in so far as social service staff are expected to undertake some assessment of the need for social work help, their role has close parallels to that of the duty officer. Unfortunately, there is little information about the extent to which a referral for a home help or for an aid can be regarded as indicative of the presence of additional problems which have not been articulated. The part played by OTs and home help organisers as referral agents for social work intervention is in need of further study.

Some work has, however, been carried out which demonstrates the value of using trained volunteers to undertake routine interviews to screen the social work and social service needs of elderly people admitted to hospital (*Going Home?*, 1975; Ricketts, 1978). The volunteer interviewers followed a questionnaire designed to seek out unexpressed need, particularly in relation to discharge arrangements. This in itself is interesting, for it represents an approach of positive out-reach to elderly people which is concerned to identify need rather than simply respond to demand. (The use of street wardens and neighbourhood workers is an example of a similar approach to elderly and other vulnerable people in the community.)

The article by Ricketts describes the attachment to a hospital social work department of volunteers, mostly in their late teens and undertaking the work as community service volunteers (CSVs). They interviewed each new admission to a geriatric unit and reported back to the social work team leader who then decided what action, if any, was required and which member of his team should become involved if intervention seemed necessary. The outcome of this use of CSVs was apparently very successful: clients' problems were identified at an earlier stage than they might otherwise have been, referrals to supplementary benefits or the area home help organiser could be passed direct to social work assistants, and qualified social workers were able to devote more time to those clients who needed their particular skills.

An important point in this system is that the two aspects of screening – gathering information and then assessing the significance of that information – were separated. The decision about how to respond to the information rested with the team leader; in other words, the social work significance was being judged by a social worker. It could be argued that a similar practice should be adopted in respect of assessments undertaken by OTs and home help organisers, thereby involving a team leader in the decision-making about when social work help is called for. In many social service teams, such a system is already in operation in respect of the reports written by duty officers and the incorporation of the OT and home help organiser assessments would subject their initial interviews to the same scrutiny accorded to those of social workers.

A separate point for consideration is whether certain referrals should routinely receive a social work assessment, irrespective of the reason for referral and in addition to a visit by, for example, a home help organiser. Recent documents on the social work task have emphasised that assessments for residential care should be undertaken by qualified social workers (Birch, 1976; British Association of Social Workers, 1977a) but that is a separate issue from the question of whether the circumstances that bring certain clients to the attention of social services require a separate social work assessment. Client vulnerability is one of the British Association of Social Workers (BASW) guidelines for allocation to a qualified social worker (BASW, 1977a). Recent bereavement, sudden severe handicap and very old age are significant indicators of vulnerability amongst old people and, taking account of this, one intake team known to the author had decided that all referrals on elderly people who had been recently bereaved or disabled should receive a social work assessment in addition to whatever else was required. After about six or eight months of this arrangement the team's perception was that they had become more involved in counselling elderly people than had been the case when it had been left to an OT or home help organiser to 'refer back'. Maybe this was because the social workers were more attuned to the subtle indicators of stress; Goldberg *et al.* (1970) found some evidence to suggest that trained social workers were more likely than the untrained to identify emotional and psychiatric problems which existed alongside the practical. Or it might have been that prior to this new system non-social work staff were unclear about the social work role. It is not, of course, unusual for people to respond to the needs of a client in terms of their own area of competence; thus a home help organiser may see the solution as more home help hours to provide company for the grieving client whereas a social worker sees it in the form of social work support and counselling. Such occupational 'tunnel vision' may have particularly unfortunate repercussions for the care of elderly clients, whose needs may be many and varied and requiring a response from more than one section within social services.

ASSESSMENT INTERVIEWS

This section considers how the conduct of assessment interviews might be shaped, first by a concern for such fundamental social work ethics as the client's right to privacy and to a confidential service and secondly by the application of knowledge about the problems that are often encountered by elderly people.

Whether the assessment is carried out by social service or social work staff, there are important ethical issues to be considered which are pertinent for interviews with clients of any age, and especially when they are vulnerable through dependency or through difficulty in making known their needs.

For every worker in the caring and helping occupations who undertakes assessments, there is the underlying question 'How far (or how "deep") should I go?'. How much information on social and emotional factors is it appropriate for home help organisers and OTs to seek? How is it to be explained to the client why these questions, which do not appear directly relevant to the request for a service, are being asked? Social workers attempting to assess the degree of risk to which confused elderly people expose themselves (and others) are faced with a particular problem about how far they should seek verification from others. Should they, for example, ask in the corner shop about the kind of food the old person buys? Should they make the client's difficulties known to others living in the community? In many ways, this is similar to the decisions faced by workers investigating suspected child abuse. Should they make inquiries of neighbours as to whether the child is left alone in the house or is heard crying for excessively long periods in the night?

The dilemma is in part a moral one: how far is it justifiable to intrude on a person's privacy, albeit with the best of motives? And it is also a professional dilemma: how far does the knowledge which is available to the worker require that he should seek information beyond that which is volunteered by the client, since to do less would be to fail in his professional responsibilities? In respect of work with elderly clients the evidence of undetected and unreported need would seem to require of the worker an understanding of the needs and difficulties commonly experienced by elderly persons so that the worker can establish whether the absence of reported need does indeed signify an absence of need.

This has obvious implications for the way in which an assessment interview is conducted. First and foremost, given that the scope may be more wide-ranging than the client might reasonably expect from the expressed reason for referral, it is important that whoever undertakes the interview does not take advantage of the willingness and indeed the eagerness of many elderly people to 'have a chat' with anyone who displays interest in their past life and present circumstances. The worker has a dual obligation here – on the one hand to seek information which will enable assessments to be accurate, and on the other to be mindful of the client's right to privacy, especially if the client is unable to safeguard himself from the attention of professionals. The role of 'someone from the welfare' is a mystery to many clients, irrespective of their age (Mayer and Timms, 1970) and clients may well be uncertain either about how far they are obliged to offer information if they want a service or about the status of an apparently friendly chat which will in fact provide the substance of a report on an official file. There will be some elderly clients whose degree of mental impairment makes it difficult, perhaps impossible, for them to understand the significance of an interview and here the worker has a particular responsibility to safeguard the client's right to confidentiality; in other, less complex cases it will be sufficient for the worker to make clear the purpose of his questions and the client's right not to answer.

Secondly, there are implications for the style of interviewing. Apart from the fact that a 'chatty' approach may mislead the client as to the purpose of the interview, the need for information of a precise nature means that questions may have to be phrased in such a way that vague or uncertain replies are kept to a minimum. Anderson (1973) discusses this point in relation to ascertaining the state of health of elderly patients. In an attempt to overcome the difficulties in reaching a diagnosis, caused by the patient's reluctance or inability to report symptoms, Anderson stresses that it may be necessary to ask precise questions which refer to the symptoms known to be common in old age and which require a 'yes/no' answer.

This point has relevance also for assessment interviews by social services department staff. Certain topics are known often to be misrepresented by elderly clients. One example, referred to earlier in the discussion of poverty, is that of adequacy of income. Accustomed to a different value of the pound, elderly persons may consider two or three hundred pounds in the bank as evidence of some wealth and their failure to claim rebates or benefit may stem from an incorrect assumption that this money makes them ineligible for help. Thus, seeking precise information about the amount in the bank (providing the client knows the object of the questioning and does not object) will provide a more accurate guide to eligibility for benefit than simply accepting the client's estimation of whether he has enough money. A second example is that an assessment of the risk of hypothermia requires information about which rooms are heated and for how long each day; in old age, an individual's sensitivity to heat and to cold decreases so the subjective feeling of being warm or cold becomes less reliable. Thirdly, precise information about when people, especially relatives, visit and from what distance is necessary to provide an accurate picture of the extent of an elderly person's contact with or isolation from the outside world. An elderly person may be reluctant to admit that he is on his own or that his family no longer has the time or inclination to visit. The presentation of an ideal picture may be a defence which could so easily be misunderstood by the interviewing social worker or home help organiser.

A final example of the importance of focused questioning concerns the assessment of mood. This is a subject which requires more attention than it has received so far. The subjective feeling of being lonely needs to be placed in the context of an elderly person's previous friendship patterns but also of his present range of contacts, some of which may seem comparatively minor – such as exchanging greetings with schoolchildren who pass – but whose regularity and reliability bring to certain parts of the day a purpose and a sense of belonging. If there are indications that the elderly person may be depressed, it is important to ascertain how far, if at all, life seems purposeless and futile. For it is this feeling, rather than one of actual unhappiness, which may point to a risk of suicide. The answer to a question such as 'Do you ever feel you wouldn't mind if you didn't wake up in the morning?' can be most revealing and it may then become appropriate to follow with questions about whether the person ever has suicidal thoughts or, as important, whether he has worked out a proper *plan* to kill himself.

The way in which questions are phrased and the manner in which they are asked may significantly influence the reply and this is one reason why knowing *what* to ask is of limited value unless it is accompanied by knowing *how* to ask. On a number of subjects (diet, visits from family, coping capacity, continence) it is to be expected that some elderly people will be reluctant to volunteer information. Or they may seek to conceal it from the interviewer and possibly also from themselves, for it is one thing to be privately aware of inadequacy, unhappiness, or discomfort and quite another to acknowledge this out loud. Some elderly people may be in social and physical circumstances about which they are somewhat ashamed, embarrassed, or frightened, and this may be their first experience of seeking help from the welfare. Thus the need for precision and rigour in interviewing should not be equated with 'mechanical' or unfeeling practice, for it demands sensitive attention to detail and to approach. In this vitally important area of practice, which is generally subject to less scrutiny in training and in supervision than it merits, there may be some lessons to be learnt from researchers who have sought information about subjects which are known to be likely to cause embarrassment or discomfiture or where there is every chance that the respondent will reply in such a way that an ideal rather than a real picture of his circumstances is described (see, for example, the account of John and Elizabeth Newson, 1968, of the way in which their interviewers found acceptable ways of asking mothers if their 4-year-old children still wet themselves during the day and night).

The sensitivity of the interviewer cannot be too heavily stressed. Judging the appropriate moment to ask certain questions, recognising when to press for further information would be to cause undue distress, gauging the physical and mental stamina of the client – these are all prerequisites of skilful interviewing. The way in which the client experiences how he is treated in these initial contacts may significantly influence the readiness with which he raises later requests for help and this is one reason why it is important that all staff concerned with assessment interviews should be competent at interviewing and not just at obtaining information.

PROFESSIONAL BOUNDARIES AND INTERPROFESSIONAL CO-OPERATION

The health and social needs of many elderly people, especially those who are very old, are often closely interrelated; hence the emphasis on the value of a multidisciplinary approach to such episodes as discharge from hospital, admission to residential care and the management of the care of those people in the community who are more severely dependent. The literature on multidisciplinary work tends to stress the advantages to be derived from sharing information, joint decision-making, obtaining feedback, and so on. Less attention is paid to how (if at all) such co-operation can be achieved (Kane, 1975). One of the few accounts of multidisciplinary work with elderly people (Fairhurst, 1977) gives an interesting account of case conferences on geriatric patients and shows that an important influence on co-operation is the clarity with which each professional or occupational group has defined its own 'territory' or area of competence. Even the apparently straightforward task of referring for routine domiciliary services can become a cause of dissension if more than one person regards this task as rightly 'his' or 'hers'.

Assessment of the needs of elderly people referred to social services departments raises some interesting questions about the breadth of the social work role and the role boundaries between, on the one hand, social work and health visiting, and, on the other, social work and occupational therapy.

It has been suggested that because health and social needs are so closely associated in old age, training for social work with elderly people should become 'para medical', thus enabling social workers to play a greater part in the assessment of health and handicap (Abrams, 1978b, p. 62). This proposed extension of the social work role would have considerable implications not just for social work practice and training but also for the future developments of health visiting and occupational therapy. Goldberg *et al.* (1970) stressed the need for social workers to be able to identify the common 'minor physical disabilities and discomforts' experienced (but often not articulated) by elderly people, but they were uncertain about the extent to which social workers should assume responsibility for the assessment of the health of their clients (pp. 198–9): 'whether this should become part of the social worker's task in close collaboration with the general practitioner or should also include a community nurse, is an open question needing further study'.

In common with a number of other recommendations for future research and discussion that the authors made, this one on the possible 'medical' role of social workers has not been explored. Nevertheless, there is little doubt that staff of social services departments do informally monitor the health needs of their elderly clients, although the reliability of their observations is uncertain.

Several studies have demonstrated that the effective way to identify the health of elderly people is for health visitors to undertake screening by using a 'properly structured proforma' (Anderson, 1973, p. 27). Indeed, Anderson (1977) argues (p. 172) that regular routine visiting by a health visitor to every person aged 70 and over 'is the only way to make an early diagnosis in the upper age range and to stop disability from worsening'.

But despite the need for early diagnosis and the proven value of such screening activities by health visitors, in practice health visitors are not widely used in relation to elderly people. For a number of reasons, almost 60 per cent of their time is at present concentrated on families with young children and their role in health education and preventive medicine has diminished as, with varying degrees of willingness, they have taken on tasks which might be regarded as rightly the responsibility of social workers (Court Report, 1976, Vol. 1). In a recent survey of elderly people in the community in England (Hunt, 1978) surveillance visiting by a member of the primary health care team was infrequent even for those elderly persons who could not take themselves to the surgery. Amongst the bedfast and housebound, slightly under four-fifths had not seen a health visitor during the past six months and just under two-thirds had not seen a district nurse; less than one-third had seen a doctor as often as once a month.

Although there is an apparent unwillingness amongst some health visitors to become more involved in work with elderly people (Hudson, 1978), it is arguably more appropriate for them to extend their health education role with this section of the population than it is for social workers to take on this aspect of work. Rather than make social work training 'para medical' it would seem more appropriate to alert social workers to the more obvious signs of possible ill-health (as usefully outlined in the BASW *Guidelines*, 1977b) and to concentrate on developing their awareness of the contributions of other relevant professionals, their ability to liaise with other agencies and their skills in direct work which might help in encouraging elderly people to make use of the preventive services that are available – an eye test every two years, for example, and a regular dental check-up. Elderly people are infrequent users of such services (Simpson, 1979) yet correct spectacles and properly fitting dentures are important aids to health and comfort.

The role boundary between social work and occupational therapy is, if anything, less clearly defined than that between social work and health visiting. In a number of social services departments, social workers and social work assistants are routinely undertaking assessments for aids and adaptations (DHSS, 1978). This is despite the statement in the *Report on the Remedial Professions* (DHSS, 1973) that 'assessment for aids is not a task appropriate to social workers'. It is also in sharp contrast to practice in the national health service, where the supply of aids is far more tightly controlled.

About seven hundred OTs work in the local authority setting, but this number is unevenly spread throughout the country and some departments either do not employ them or are considerably understaffed. It is difficult to overestimate the seriousness of this shortage of OTs which affects the quality of life of mentally ill and mentally handicapped people as well as those who are physically disabled.

The image of OTs as craft workers has slowly been replaced by that of 'aids and adaptations' people, but there is a part of their role which is probably less widely understood yet which contains the potential for considerable overlap with activities central to social work. This concerns the role of the OT in counselling people who are disabled. Some OTs would argue that their para medical training and their training in counselling (which forms part of their course) enable them to be more effective than social workers in helping clients come to terms with disability and some measure of dependency. The role of social workers with physically disabled clients of all ages is itself undeveloped and this, together with the heavy workloads of social workers and OTs, may reduce the likelihood of competition between them for clients for whom each claims responsibility. However, disputes may still arise; for example, if the OT undertakes to counsel a client or family in connection with the onset of disability, does this include dealing with the child who exhibits delinquent behaviour some six months after his father became partially paralysed? Consideration of the boundaries of occupational therapy in conjunction with those of social work should form the basis of the proposed development of each profession within the local authority.

Clarity about respective roles is therefore an essential part of successful interprofessional co-operation. There will always be some degree of overlap and flexibility between workers in associated professions or occupations and it is to the benefit of clients and of workers that this should be. But this is very different from confused and maybe conflicting expectations about responsibilities and expertise which may result in duplication of effort or failure to act on the mistaken assumption that the task in question 'belonged to' someone else. Greater exchange between health visitors, OTs and social workers about their perceptions of each other and also about the framework of knowledge and the theory that they bring to their work would be of benefit. On the one hand, this would encourage all three professions to identify the direction to be taken in the future development of their roles. Such awareness is as important in times of retrenchment as it is in times of expansion. On the other hand, it would be valuable to explore both the differences and the similarities of approach to certain problems. The questions a social worker might 'automatically' ask of a client in a given situation may differ from those of a health visitor or OT in the same situation and vice versa. But equally, there are likely to be some questions that they all ask. Identification of the common ground as well as of the discrete areas of specialist concern could contribute to greater expertise in the task of assessment, thereby serving the needs of a variety of different professional interests as well as those of the client.

Chapter 5

Elderly People Living Alone

The majority of elderly people in England (about two-thirds) live either on their own or with an elderly spouse. There are, as is to be expected, considerable variations between age-groups, so that the proportion living alone increases with increasing age. Just over two-fifths of those aged 85 and over live on their own – the combination of their advanced age and their solitary living circumstances making them a particularly vulnerable section of the elderly population. Amongst the most severely dependent of the elderly population, there is a small proportion who live alone: approximately 8 per cent of those who cannot get to the lavatory unaided and 9 per cent of those who cannot get in and out of bed without help are on their own and a quarter of those who are bedfast or housebound are similarly dependent on outside helpers (Hunt, 1978).

Whilst visiting relatives provide an important source of help to elderly people living alone or with an elderly spouse, there are some old people who have few family supports. One elderly person in twenty has no living close relative and a further one in twenty never receives visits from relatives. Not surprisingly, the very old, who are likely to be the most handicapped, are also the most likely to have either no close relatives or relatives who are themselves too infirm to undertake visiting.

Wasser (1966) has emphasised that family relationships are important to an elderly person on account not just of the quality of those currently experienced but also of the significance of those that have been lost or perhaps never enjoyed. An elderly person on his own may express bitterness at being abandoned, as he sees it, by members of his family who have not maintained contact. Or his gradually increasing need for care may reawaken his sense of loss at being childless or without children who have survived to look after him. He may dwell, at times quite unrealistically, on the ways in which life would have been different if only a much-loved (and by implication much-loving) son or daughter had been available to provide care. In a similar manner, some children in care have been known to invest their parents with almost fairy godmother powers. Being alone may be a source of pain which is easily revealed, as a social worker found out: 'I've become very conscious of my ability to hurt old people [in hospital] by simple things like asking "have you had any letters or visitors?".' Home helps might also come across similar examples: 'We have quite a lot of difficulty with some of our clients on Monday mornings when perhaps they have seen their neighbour being visited by her daughter and taken out for lunch on Sunday but their own family doesn't come ...'

Social workers and home helps may at times be 'adopted' by a client who is seeking a substitute family. The following quotation illustrates this; the social worker was about the same age as the client's daughter who apparently made only the most perfunctory visits to her now-widowed mother:

> I've got a lady, I still go and see her and I can't see I shall ever not be seeing her now. I had her husband for about 4½ years, he'd had a stroke and I used to go and talk to him on the ward, though he couldn't talk back, and if his wife was visiting I'd have a word with her too ... He went home and came back for several short stays and then he had further strokes [and] died but I carried on seeing his wife ... I don't go very often now, perhaps every six weeks or when I'm in the street, but she says 'You will come again, won't you, you won't leave me now, I can't do without you and him'. I question what I'm doing but I feel I can't opt out and it doesn't do me any harm to go in for half an hour or so ... Maybe if I was [a different age] there wouldn't be the same feeling there ...

Clearly the relationship which had developed here between client and worker was influenced by the fact that the worker was an important link between the client's past and the present; the worker had also been with the client during times of great stress following her husband's strokes and then when he was dying in hospital. It was not surprising that the bond between the two was a close one. Yet in that account the social worker conveys her uncertainty as to the purpose and value of her visits, founded on an unease that it is in some way inappropriate. This is a difficult issue, and one faced by many social workers with clients who, like some old people, feel on their own in the world. Young children in care may ask the question outright – 'Will you be my daddy now?' – but adults may pose the question more obliquely. Goldberg *et al*. (1970, p. 198) noted that 'in working with the old, the case worker is more likely to slip into the role of a substitute son or daughter or grandchild' and this can, of course, be used in a variety of ways. Social workers who are in their twenties may find that 'playing at grandchild' is an easy way of avoiding some of the more difficult problems presented by the client. On the other hand, the elderly person may act out previous parental or grandparental relationships in the relationship with the social worker and this transference has the potential to impede as well as to facilitate the help to be offered.

Wasser (1966, p. 46) also describes how the social worker can become 'a very special person' to a client who has experienced many losses and may as a result be deprived of part of his identity. She continues that the role of family substitute or the assumption of a 'social' role 'must not be perceived as a threat to [the worker's] professional competence but as an added dimension which involves use of the caseworker's most useful tool: the relationship between client and worker'. However, it seems important that the forms of caring that a social worker might provide in the absence of family or friends – help with moving to a new home, comfort during illness, or admission to hospital, for example – should normally be of a temporary nature, paving the way to the introduction of additional supportive relationships which gradually decrease the client's dependence on the worker. As Goldberg *et al*. (1970) pointed out, the long-term needs of friendship and support are usually more appropriately provided by volunteers, neighbours and the like, for social workers rarely have the time to accept the responsibility that is inherent in establishing a permanent relationship with a client. The skill of the social worker lies in maintaining the balance between the 'social' and the 'professional' elements of the role and in knowing how and when to introduce others who might more appropriately meet the needs for friendship and social contact.

In their study of the work of the Task Force Volunteers, Hadley *et al*. (1975, p. 191) found that 'it is clearly not impossible to help old people develop substitutes or compensate for relationships they have lost or never had'. The potential for volunteers to become a meaningful part of an old person's life has been demonstrated elsewhere (Kent Community Care Project, 1979) but in many instances it is unrealistic to expect this to happen given the somewhat haphazard way in which voluntary help is used by many social workers (Holme and Maizels, 1978). Practice within the Kent Community Care Project may offer valuable guidelines as to how the relationship between a paid volunteer and, in this case, an elderly person can best be initiated. A project worker (who is a social worker) establishes with the volunteer and the elderly person the task(s) to be carried out and through joint discussions the role and expectations of all parties concerned (including the project) are clarified and made explicit. The purpose is thereby to establish a basic level of involvement, but from this there is the opportunity for 'extras' to develop with a degree of spontaneity as client and volunteer get to know each other and if they wish this to happen; the relationship between them can be shaped according to the inclinations and capacities of each, in a manner similar to the normal process of developing an acquaintanceship or friendship. It is, of course, not unusual for home helps to offer in a similar way additional services and social contact beyond those for which they are paid.

The presence in the community of a group of dependent elderly people living on their own or with another elderly person who is also infirm places heavy demands on domiciliary health and social services. In one area of a social services department, one-quarter of all elderly clients – mostly those who were very old – received four or more services (Avon, 1977). That the most dependent elderly people consume a large proportion of domiciliary services is to be expected and suggests that those in most need receive most help. However, this concentration of resources on some people may have implications for the provision to others who need help but not so urgently. It is those with the less extreme needs who are increasingly refused service when resources do not keep pace with demand (Opit, 1977; Mooney, 1978).

A major difficulty in meeting the needs of dependent elderly people who live alone is that their needs are not always predictable and may, therefore, not coincide with the essentially episodic care offered by visiting relatives or domiciliary services.

Most patients in Isaacs' (1971) study of 280 admissions to a geriatric unit had received at least some support from relatives, neighbours or domiciliary services; but (p. 283):

> the trouble usually was that their needs were not met during part of the day or night. This was most often the case with patients who fell and remained lying on the floor all night till someone came to the door in the morning, or who soiled themselves.

Goldberg *et al*. (1978, p. 286) commented in similar fashion when they questioned the efficacy of the 'occasional social work visit' as 'the most appropriate means of providing support or of anticipating approaching crises' amongst the very frail elderly people known to an area team; in just over two-thirds of these surveillance cases, an unforeseen crisis occurred before the next review visit was due. Similar examples of the difficulty in providing adequate surveillance can be found in the management of child abuse cases.

Clearly, therefore, it is not just the quantity but also the organisation of services which is important. The Kent Community Care Project is one experiment in the development of neighbourhood networks which can provide support that is individually tailored to a particular person's needs. An intensive domiciliary care scheme in Hove (Dunnachie, 1979) employs care assistants to work, not in a residential setting, but in the elderly person's own home, and the initial stages of this scheme seem to indicate that admission to care or to hospital can be delayed at a cost considerably below that of maintaining a person in either form of institutional care. It would seem that the Hove scheme enables very frail elderly people who do not wish to enter care and who do not require constant attention through twenty-four hours to be adequately supported in the community. Several short visits a day rather than a single block of time seem to be required and for this reason either the care assistants have to live near their elderly clients or, as in Hove, they require their own transport. The role of the social worker attached to the scheme is interesting, incorporating three main areas of work: advising on housing and benefits, helping isolated elderly people to cope with loss and bereavement and acting as one of the sources of support available to the care assistants. It would seem that caring for the carers could become an increasingly important part of social work if neighbourhood and community schemes become more widely developed.

A third example of an attempt to meet the unpredictable demand for services which a very dependent elderly person may require comes from Stockport where some of the most vulnerable elderly persons are provided with a 'communication box' which connects them to a control centre and thence to a team of wardens who drive radio-controlled cars. The wardens can make routine calls at regular intervals during the day – and night if necessary – and also answer emergency requests for help. Apart from providing the means to summon help, the box in each person's home is also sensitive to smoke, and to extremes of hot or cold, and sends signals to the control centre if smoke or extremes of room temperature are detected (Stockport Social Services Department, 1978).

The Kent, Hove and Stockport schemes are three examples of attempts to provide for quite severely dependent frail elderly people a level of community care which offers a realistic and acceptable alternative to care in an institution. In this sense, therefore, these schemes increase the choices open to people who require care; as Moroney (1976) stresses, choice cannot properly be said to exist unless the options available are comparable one with the other. Care of the dependent elderly population is one example where the choices open to them may be limited or possibly non-existent, as when a person enters residential care because domiciliary services provide a level of care insufficient to his needs or, alternatively, he continues to live in the community on the waiting list for the residential care he has requested. Both the quantity and the quality of the alternatives are significant if they are to be viewed as options which are equally possible.

PROTECTION AND RISK

A central issue in the management of dependency is the management of risk. This is a complex matter of concern to all caretakers – be they professionals employed to work in long-term care facilities or in the community, or be they neighbours, friends, or relatives of the dependent person. In many instances, too, coping with risk will be an everyday experience for the dependent person himself. The balance between safety and danger, security and risk is a delicate one, involving an assessment of type and level of risk; both of these may be differently perceived by the various parties involved. In addition, there may be no uniformity in the definition of what constitutes 'acceptable' risk. The dilemma for social workers and other care staff in social services departments is well expressed in the following quotation which comes from a social worker in an intake team: 'the GP, neighbours or the family say to us "But this person is at risk, he might fall". And that's true, he *might* fall. So what should be done?'

The risks to which people are exposed or to which they expose themselves may be emotional, psychological, or physical. As a general rule, these three types are placed in a hierarchy, with physical risk assuming the greatest importance, possibly because it is easier to assess and the preservation of life is a fundamental concern. Yet there is a subtle and complex relationship between the three, not just because the preservation of life must lead to questions about the quality of life but because there is an interdependence which has yet to be fully understood. Thus one old person in the community who is gradually becoming more neglectful of herself and is overburdened by the demands of self-care may find that the certainty of care in an elderly person's home decreases her level of anxiety and insecurity. On the other hand, moving an elderly client into an environment where physical risk is less apparent may present a serious threat to psychological well-being and this may, in turn, contribute to the death of the client in the period immediately following admission. The vulnerability of old people would appear to lie as much in the interdependence of physical, emotional and psychological factors as it does in the significance of any one of those in isolation.

The perception of risk and the assessment of severity will be influenced by, for example, the amount of knowledge available to each concerned and by the rewards of taking some risks weighed against the unavoidable disadvantages. The risk of falling or of being ill alone in the night may be accepted by some elderly people because the value of being in their own home in a familiar neighbourhood is considered more important. This is not to say that the risks will be ignored or that there will be no anxiety about what might happen in the event of an emergency; rather, the old

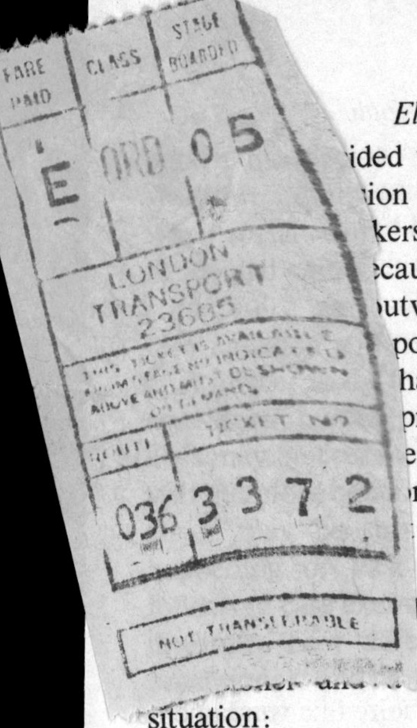

ided that the risks are 'worth it', but may still ion about how to manage them. In a similar kers may encourage an old person to enter ecause they regard the risks of remaining in the outweighing the risks of institutionalisation, possible death after admission.

hat may affect the assessment of risk is that the professional may differ from that by another. e one has more knowledge than the other and re aware of the possibilities and probabilities. there is a misunderstanding of what is of clarity about each other's roles. The ple (given from a social worker's perspective) rent professionals – in this case a general social worker – may perceive the same situation:

> A brother and sister, both in their eighties, lived together, the sister being physically and emotionally dependent on her brother. He was then admitted to hospital and found to be seriously ill and may never be fit for discharge. The GP saw the sister as at risk but we arranged intensive domiciliary services, using the home help to teach and encourage the sister to look after herself and not to give up. But the GP saw what we were doing as not doing anything and to ensure that something *was* done he admitted the old lady to hospital. The progress we think she had made with home help now seems likely to be undone; we doubt if she'll ever return home now.

Whatever the appropriateness or otherwise of the actions taken by the social worker and by the general practitioner (and the latter's interpretation of the case is not known), several important questions are raised about the nature of each profession's responsibility and accountability. This is not, of course, purely a matter for debate between professionals but also within each individual – witness the difficulty that medical practitioners sometimes have in deciding whether a mentally ill old person 'belongs' to the psychiatrist or the geriatrician. However, in the case that has been quoted, the social worker had defined the degree of risk and, considering it to be acceptable, had initiated a programme of intervention; the general practitioner had apparently found the degree of risk unacceptable and the social worker's intervention inappropriate and had acted according to his own professional judgement. In the circumstances, it could be argued that had he failed to do this he would have been failing in his own obligations to his patient. But in so doing he effectively ended the social work 'treatment'. Where does responsibility lie and who is accountable when more than one profession is concerned with the client, they are not in a hierarchical relationship to each other and yet they can intervene in such a way as to 'cut across' each other's work? These questions need more careful study if multidisciplinary work in respect of the elderly is to become more widely developed.

The tolerance of risk, whether by client, worker, or both, carries with it acceptance of the inherent anxiety. For the elderly person this might range from the worry caused by forgetfulness or the prospect that he *might* forget something (Abrams, 1978b) through to the fear of being unable to attract help if he were taken ill. For the social worker there is the feeling that, whatever the support offered by senior staff, in the final analysis responsibility lies with him (DHSS, 1978). The strength of this feeling, and the confusion that surrounds the meanings of responsibility and accountability, make for difficulty in clarifying the extent to which senior staff can be expected to encourage or even to permit their subordinates to take the risks which may be important, possibly crucial, if the client is to be allowed any control over different aspects of his life.

Much of the debate about acceptable levels of risk focuses on the more extreme examples where the life of the client or those around him may be in danger and compulsory admission to psychiatric hospital or to residential care is being considered. However, the less dramatic instances are no less significant because of the effect they may have on the quality of life that is to be enjoyed. The following example comes from a social worker who organised outings for a group of isolated elderly people. It illustrates the process by which this social worker had worked out and continued to work out the basis for her decision in the light of questions for which there is no certain answer.

> [The people in my group] want to be taken out. More than anything else they like a drive, maybe only for an hour or so, nothing much. But getting them in and out of coaches – really I was terrified. But I've

now come round to thinking that if they die when they're out, they are dying doing what they wanted to do. But I have been very frightened and when I've seen them go a funny colour, I've really been apprehensive in a big way ... but I've come to accept that they are all going to die some time and they may as well die happy. I don't know whether that's right or not ... We all occasionally do things that we know we're going to pay for afterwards, don't we, and I say to them 'Well look, do you really feel you should go, the road may be bumpy and twisty' and if they say 'Yes, I want to', then all right. I try to think would I have let my mother do it, what would my mother have done? That's the main thing I've got to fall back on and then, if it makes them happy, in the main I say all right.

Social workers may well be involved in helping other people to cope with anxieties about the apparent vulnerability of an elderly person. A family might urge a recently bereaved relative to accept residential care rather than to see if it is possible to cope alone, albeit with support; allowing the old person time on his own may seem to the family to demonstrate a lack of caring. Or a very disabled or disordered elderly person may be determined to remain in his own home, despite obvious risks to his own and possibly also other people's health and safety. Part of the social worker's role may be to protect the elderly person's right to take such risks; this may involve taking the pressure from other people concerned with the client, dealing with their anxieties and maybe anger, justifying what may appear to be unwarranted inactivity by the refusal to persuade the client to enter care and at the same time constantly reviewing the client's situation to ensure that the risk to the client and to others has not become too great. The following quotation illustrates the many tasks involved.

One of my clients, a frail old lady, was admitted to hospital after a fall. She lives in very primitive housing conditions and a niece is very much involved with her. There is a good deal of pressure from neighbours and other people to have this old lady rehoused or admitted to Part III [residential care] but she does not wish for this. I see my involvement because of the pressure to 'do something' about the old lady, also to support the niece and pick up the number of different phone calls, letters, etc., which regularly come in about the client ...

A similar supportive role may sometimes be appropriate with

home helps and home help organisers who are faced with clients whose level of frailty seems to require more care than the client is prepared to accept.

The second part of the social worker's role lies in the creation and maintenance of what has been described as a 'prosthetic environment' (Wasser, 1971). This can vary considerably – from the apparently simple but quite effective arrangements that can be made between neighbours to indicate that help is required ('If Mrs Baker's curtains are not pulled back by 10 o'clock, I go over to see if she is all right') – to the more complex system of providing aids and regular, routine visits by domiciliary care staff, voluntary visitor and field social worker. Wasser also emphasises the importance of developing a 'stand-by plan' which may be put into effect should circumstances suddenly deteriorate.

Some American research on the effectiveness of developing care networks offers an important cautionary lesson (Blenkner *et al.*, 1971). The researchers noted (p. 495) that in their study:

> the primary finding with regard to institutionalisation is that service increases its likelihood. Despite the availability of an ancillary home aide service program, it appears that the well-trained social worker who is assigned responsibility for the welfare of older people has a strong tendency to move them into 'protective settings'.

The consequences for the client of being 'noticed' by the professionals may thus be far-reaching. It has been suggested that the professional feels the pressure to 'do something' in order to protect himself from public criticism in the event of a tragedy; or that he responds to society's need to limit and control the extent to which a person's life deviates from current norms. However, it may also be a function of a powerful desire to protect vulnerable human beings and to demonstrate caring for and about people; the question 'Could I or should I do more?' is prompted by concern for the other person and not just by concern to 'cover' oneself.

An aspect of risk-taking which receives rather less attention is how to help clients to manage risks or encourage them to take more. An obvious example of the latter concerns the stroke patient who is afraid to extend the limits of function because the blow to his confidence or the fear of another stroke has made him unwilling to contemplate taking any chances. An unexpectedly debilitating illness, a fall, or an admission to hospital can also pose a very real threat to a client's coping mechanisms, even when physical recovery is excellent. This quotation demonstrates the importance of the social worker's attention to detail and the step-by-step nature of the interview in which the client, an in-patient, is encouraged to consider discharge home:

> Well, you discuss how they could let someone know they needed help. Have they got a neighbour? Can they put a card in the window? Then, does the neighbour come round, so that twice a day there is somebody who will keep an eye on the house and they won't feel so lonely? And you say you will go home with them, and reassure them that the door can be properly locked, that they can manage to lock it. You say you'll ask the OT to call to see if any adaptations can be done and to make sure they can get in and out of bed, that the commode is in the right place for them. It's reassuring them and it's a long, slow job but you can't rush them ... very often you can be with them for half an hour and everything appears normal and then, suddenly, they will confide in you and tell you their fears and worries ...

The importance of a precise exploration of the risks experienced by the client has been described by Cormican (1977) in the context of task-centred work with elderly clients. Cormican describes working with an elderly client over a two-month period to make the client's flat where she lived 'accident-proof': this involved the client making a list of all the activities that made her feel weak and dizzy and exploring with the worker the ways in which these might be avoided. Client and worker also found a satisfactory way of making sure that daily telephone contact was established between the client and an outside person. One of the values of a joint exercise of this kind is that it directly involves the client with his environment and enables him, with help, to achieve some control over it. For people who have become frail, this opportunity to make decisions and to master certain aspects of their life is of vital importance. Moreover, it offers a much-needed chance to succeed at something when their life might seem to be one currently filled with failures.

It is significant that on a number of occasions in this chapter social work involvement has been part of a wider 'package' of support in which volunteers, domiciliary care staff and the like provide an equally important contribution; indeed it may well be that they, rather than the social worker, are more frequently in contact with the elderly person concerned. Were there more OTs in the local authority, one could see a major role for them, especially where the concern is to create a prosthetic environment.

A second point to note is the attention to basic daily living activities which is often required of the worker who is helping an elderly person manage living alone. The focus is on the practical as well as the emotional significance of frailty and disability – both of which are likely to be closely associated.

Finally, where the elderly person is physically or mentally very frail, there are difficult questions about intervention – what type, how much, when, if at all. Decisions of this kind are not unique to work with elderly clients but they figure more prominently than in many other aspects of social work practice. The process of managing risks needs more careful analysis, from the point of view of the agency, the worker, the client, the client's friends, family or neighbours and the other professionals who are involved. For, as Wasser (1971) remarks with such cogency, if the purpose of intervention is to help the client survive, care must be taken to ensure that he is not destroyed in the process.

Chapter 6

Care by the Family

Most studies of parent–child relationships, of sibling relationships and of family interaction have focused on the nuclear family of parents and their young children; the nature of the relationships between adult children and their ageing parents, between adult siblings and between grandparents and their grandchildren has received less attention. Yet the complexity of family life stems from the interaction, over time, of relationships both within and between generations. Such relationships are strengthened or weakened as they are redefined in response to changing needs and circumstances.

The extent to which these are different for each generation at different stages of experience is made very clear in the following (Kirschner, 1979, p. 209): 'At a time when the [elderly] parent needs help adjusting to the aging process, the adult children are facing the problems of menopause, the climacteric and retirement; grandchildren are experiencing the difficulties of adolescence or new marriages; great-grandchildren are being born and are claiming the attention of the family.' The important point here is that the different stages occur at the same time, providing new opportunities for fulfilment and co-operation and also for competition and the re-enactment of former conflicts. Although some families may be geographically separated, there is little evidence that their emotional bonds have weakened; nevertheless, communication by letter, telephone, or the occasional short visit imposes its own constraints on sharing and understanding and the management of being 'a family' which is divided by distance poses particular problems.

Simos (1973, p. 78) has stated that 'the aging of an individual eventually results in a crisis for every family'. (The word 'crisis' is used here in the literal sense of a 'decisive moment' rather than in the colloquial sense of moment of disaster.) Her reasons for this can be seen as twofold. On the one hand, the normal ageing of a parent faces the adult child with a change in the child–parent relationship. Formerly it was the parent who was depended upon and who seemed always to be there; now the adult child has to learn to accept that the permanence is not a reality and that he must assume the role of the dependable person – the 'filial role' as Blenkner (1965) describes it. As was made evident earlier, this reworking of the parent–child relationship takes place at a time when much else is also happening within the family and the adult child may find himself pulled in several directions. Moreover, his capacity to resolve his changing relationship with his ageing parent is likely to influence the course of his relationships with other significant members of his family and, in turn, to be influenced by them.

On the other hand, the crisis of ageing may assume a more obvious significance for a family if the ageing parent becomes sufficiently frail that decisions have to be made about a move to a more protected environment. Wasser (1966, p. 13) has noted 'the changed interaction among family members that results from the impact of an aged person's decline' and this is well illustrated in the account by Simos (1973) of the degree of involvement of adult children in their ageing parents' physical and psychological problems: taking them to medical appointments, ensuring medication was appropriately taken, offering certain protective and supportive services, providing comfort, consolation and companionship. The worry of the adult children over their frail elderly parents and the attempts that are made to find a solution may also affect grandchildren whose position once-removed from the immediacy of caring allows them the opportunity to observe how their parents treat *their* parents. Added to this, relationships with aunts and uncles may become strained if there are tensions between the adult siblings over who 'cares' (both literally and figuratively) for their ageing parent(s). Grandchildren may feel acutely aware of divided loyalties in seeing on the one hand the obvious distress of their parents, aunts and uncles and on the other the equally unhappy position of their grandparents (Streltzer, 1979).

THE EXTENT OF CARING

Despite the widespread popular belief that families no longer care, or do not care enough, about their elderly relatives, a major part of the community care of dependent elderly people is undertaken by their families, be this in the form of episodic help with shopping or housework, temporary care during periods of acute illness, or permanent care when an elderly person has become very frail or disabled. The willingness of families to provide a home for their very dependent elderly relatives was commented on by Lowther and Williamson (1966), whose study of discharges from a geriatric unit led them to conclude that 'there is no evidence of extensive unwillingness amongst relatives to accept home care of the aged'. On the contrary, they noted that relatives tended to be 'unreasonably' willing to assume care when, on the assessment of unit staff, the degree of dependency in the old person justified the provision of permanent hospital care. A similar picture emerged from the study by Isaacs and Neville (1976) whose findings draw attention also to the level of dependency which exists in the community; the results of their research (p. 64):

> seem to indicate that substantially more old people with symptoms of dependency were cared for at home than in hospital. For every immobile old person in the present sample who was in hospital there were two at home; for every two incontinent persons in hospital there were three at home; and for every three with severe mental abnormality there were four at home ... These figures suggest that the greater part of the care of dependent old people in the survey fell upon their relatives, including spouses, others of the same generation and children; and that hospital beds were used preferentially for those who lived alone and who had no close relatives.

When an elderly person has become very dependent, the sheer amount of physical care or the constant watchfulness that may be required places enormous demands on the physical as well as the emotional stamina of those providing care. But the evidence that exists indicates that old people and their carers continue trying to cope until, to use Isaacs' apposite terminology, they are indeed 'defeated'.

Some attempts have been made to analyse the factors associated with the breakdown of family care. Certain aspects of caring may cause particular difficulty – Sanford (1975) found that faecal incontinence and sleep disturbance placed particularly heavy demands on the carer's tolerance. Some manifestations of dementia may cause the carer more distress than others. The authors of an article describing a support group for relatives caring for demented elderly people (Fuller *et al.*, 1979) noted that incontinence was generally something 'to be borne philosophically' but if a demented person packed to go home when already at home, or accused the carer of lying, stealing, and not caring, this caused great distress (p. 1684); 'these themes were amongst the most emotionally painful and tragic occurring within the setting of dementia. The group could give comfort but the wounds were deep.' (It is interesting to note that the attitude towards incontinence differed from that in Sanford's study, suggesting not that one study must be 'wrong' but rather that different carers will experience different kinds of strain.)

Philip Abrams (1977) commented (p. 141) on the 'extremely detailed even trivial' nature of many of the individual stresses of caring which, because they occur day after day, have a powerful cumulative effect. An elderly person's habits and rituals assume a different significance when brought into a family with its own ways of living; without his own home and many of his possessions, the habits of a lifetime may become especially important to an elderly person who has few other reminders of his identity left. Yet his attempts to retain these habits may seem like stubbornness; the sense of loss at losing his home may not be understood as a bereavement and instead the sadness and restlessness seem like ingratitude for the care being provided (Simos, 1973). The 'costs' of caring must be measured not just in terms of the more extreme examples of strife and family breakdown but in the enforced restrictions on the social life of many carers, the chronic misery caused by persistent loss of sleep and the threat to the physical and mental health of the carer (Sainsbury and Grad, 1971; Sanford, 1975). It is not that the care required is necessarily highly skilled – rather that it must be constantly provided.

The experience of caring brings to the fore the conflicting responses to being depended upon which were outlined in an earlier chapter. At an individual level, each carer will find different satisfactions and strains. The intensity of parent–child relationships, embedded in a long family history, heightens all the emotions that would normally be present. It may well be that what one can do for one's children one cannot do for one's parent; that the closeness of family relationships makes the performance of intimate care tasks fraught with embarrassment and discomfort; or that what one can do without question for one's own parents one cannot do for parents-in-law. The provision of support services may not always be the answer: an incontinence laundry service is of very limited help if the fundamental problem is that a daughter-in-law cannot bring herself to clean and change her mother-in-law. Caring for a severely dependent person of any age can bring the care-giver to the limits of his capacity to provide adequate personal care and the realisation of this is likely to bring considerable guilt, sadness and possibly also anger at being thus tested and found to be wanting.

THE POSSIBILITY OF ABUSE

Given the strain which many carers are experiencing, it is to be expected that exasperation and at times anger will occasionally erupt. This may at times follow well-intentioned behaviour from the elderly person whose wish to be helpful is rejected because of other pressures on the carer. A social worker gave the following example:

> Arthritics are very, very slow and they'll go into the kitchen with their walking aid ... And the daughter or daughter-in-law is trying to get a meal and it's 'What shall I do, dear?'. And the daughter is in a hurry, she wants to put a pan down or something and the old lady is tottering through ... Then if the old person is difficult as well as being slow, well ...

Physical and emotional abuse of elderly people by their adult children has yet to be considered with the same degree of urgency as the abuse of children or of wives. Yet, as Steinmetz (1978) points out (p. 54):

> There are several parallels between the battered child and battered parent. First, both are in a dependent position – relying on their caretakers for basic survival needs. Second, both are presumed protected by virtue of the love, gentleness and caring which we assume that the family provides. A third point is that both the

> dependent child and the dependent elderly adult can be a source of emotional, physical and financial stress to the caretaker.

Steinmetz is writing of the position as she sees it in the United States – and it is interesting that several other American writers also comment on the financial strain of caring which is experienced by many American families. The attendance allowance and the national health service (for all its undoubted shortcomings in geriatric medicine) may ease the financial burden on families in the United Kingdom, but the other points mentioned by Steinmetz are as relevant here as they are in the United States.

It is impossible to know the frequency with which abuse of elderly parents occurs. Very few examples at present come to light and those that do tend to be the most extreme – a prosecution for wilful neglect or allegations that a wealthy elderly person had been 'persuaded' to alter her will. What remains uncertain is the extent of emotional abuse (shouting, verbal abuse, or the exclusion of the elderly person from conversation and activities) and the carelessness or insensitivity which may sometimes be unintentional which may result in accidents: frail elderly persons may easily fall if someone brushes past impatiently or simply makes them anxious and flustered by trying to get them to hurry. The strain on some carers may indeed bring them to the limits of their self-control.

Examples of ill-treatment can, of course, be found in some institutional settings and it is also true that abuse may come from elderly persons themselves. At times, this may be a consequence of dementia or of a stroke or it may represent the norm for that person who throughout his life has tended to be aggressive and irascible. Being dependent may also provoke a violent reaction from within the disabled person and walking sticks or wheelchairs can make very effective weapons. But, given what is known about the potential for violent behaviour between husbands and wives and between parents and young children, it is reasonable to suppose that severely dependent elderly parents are similarly at risk of abuse from their adult children who care for them. Moreover, like many battered wives, abused elderly people may be reluctant to leave the tense and unhappy family home, perhaps because they fear the unknown or are ashamed of what has taken place (Steinmetz, 1978). The following case illustration demonstrates the level of feeling in a family, the paucity of choices facing the elderly person, her denial and the extent to which the family as a whole is locked in misery. The social worker is describing an evening visit where she was trying to reconcile her elderly client's refusal of any form of short-term or permanent care with the relatives' professed inability to continue to provide physical care:

> I had a difficult discussion with Mrs Jenkins and her relatives, at the end of which Mrs Jenkins said, 'You don't want me, do you, but you won't say so.' One relative said angrily, 'No, we don't want you' to which Mrs Jenkins replied, 'Well, I'll go now then, I'll get a taxi.' I asked where she could go – 'Anywhere, to my friends, anywhere,' she said. But she didn't go – indeed there was nowhere where she could go. Next morning I went to see her in the day hospital to talk about care; I asked her 'How are things?' She said firmly, 'Quite all right now, dear, everything's fine.' But I spoke to her relatives and they are still adamant that they want her to leave ... I don't know the answer to this one really. Maybe her relatives will throw her out – that would be painful for her but maybe for the best in the long run.

Whilst examples of such apparently irreconcilable conflict between old people and their carers may be rare and it is important not to get the matter out of porportion, nevertheless the possibility of violence as a reaction to stress cannot be ignored. But, as in many instances of child abuse, the details will not emerge unless the carer is questioned specifically on the subject. Violent feelings towards one's parents are perhaps less easy to acknowledge than are those against one's children, where publicity has done much to make people aware of the potential for abuse. For this reason, the social worker may well have to take the initiative in exploring the possibility of abuse; and the questions will need to be phrased in such a way that the carer understands that it is a subject which is permissible for discussion.

HELPING THE CARING FAMILY

A not uncommon complaint from social workers is that referrals on families caring for a dependent elderly person come 'too late' when attitudes and patterns of behaviour have become settled and the point of desperation has been reached on one or both sides. Isaacs (1971) observed that referral to a geriatric unit contained similar characteristics of emergency or at least urgency (pp. 125–6): 'In almost two-thirds of the cases accepted for the geriatric unit, referral to hospital was delayed until the patient lacked the basic elements of care [insufficient food, warmth, cleanliness and safety] or until the help which he obtained ... threatened to break down.'

One of the difficulties, of course, is in defining how 'early' such referrals should be received or, possibly, sought out by social workers and health visitors; if the health needs of people over 70 or over 75 were routinely screened, this might prove one way in which family strain could be detected before chronic misery results in the breakdown of care. Moroney (1976) has argued that the state has always tended to leave families to cope on their own with their dependent elderly relatives, only providing help when breakdown or 'defeat' is imminent. The notion of a 'partnership' between welfare services and the caring relative has been little developed; the level of provision of day care services varies considerably from one authority to another and the use of night sitters, where they are employed, is usually limited to caring for the terminally ill. The concentration of domiciliary services on those elderly people living alone or with another elderly person has been noted in studies which examined the distribution of home help and home care services (Goldberg and Connelly, 1978). The question 'What is the relative's equivalent of the nurse's time off?' (Philip Abrams, 1977) has yet to receive sufficient attention.

The unremitting nature of the care that is required by some elderly people becomes of even greater significance when one examines *who* cares. In his analysis of referrals to a geriatric unit, Isaacs (1971) found that in the 141 examples where the amount and nature of care had imposed severe strain on the carers, in all but one case the main burden of care fell on one person. These 'principal helpers' were usually an adult child, the spouse, or another family member and nearly three-quarters were aged 50 or over. Similarly, in the Cumbrian town they studied, Butcher and Crosbie (1977, p. 105) noted that 'there is normally only one child who lives sufficiently close to the parent to be of help in times of stress and difficulty'.

The provision of short-term residential care or 'holiday' care can offer carers valuable relief but what is often lacking is routine but flexible arrangements which would allow relatives to go out for a day, a few hours or for a night without applying months in advance and without receiving 'blocks' of relief which, while welcome, do not offer on-going support. Sanford (1975) noted that the relatives he interviewed welcomed the idea of a 'granny sitter' service (p. 473): 'this was a real unfulfilled need'.

The importance of receiving relief from the long-term physical strain of caring cannot be overestimated. Many carers will not receive this until the elderly person has to be admitted to hospital perhaps following a fall or an acute illness; at this point the freedom from caring may make the carer realise the enormity of the burden he has been bearing and he may be understandably reluctant to consider resuming such a task. The very few cases of refusals to care have to be understood in the light of past relationships and present needs for care, and a social worker is well placed to explore with the carer the meaning of the caring role. Where there is outright and adamant rejection of the elderly person, one must seek the reason why the carer or potential carer has assumed such an intransigent stand. Is it because any sign of indecision might be 'exploited' by the professionals who have their own pressures and responsibilities?

The social worker may be in a position of considerable influence over discharge arrangements and the amount of persuasion that should be exerted. The decisions to be made are sometimes difficult, as a hospital social worker described:

> Sometimes you try and achieve a change of attitude, but it takes a lot of doing in many cases and I sometimes question whether it's the right thing to do ... You can see the doctor's point that there is nothing more he can do for the patient who needs the right care in the community but ... you can also put yourself in the relative's or the friend's position and think, well am I right to try and persuade them to go on caring as they were before ... And sometimes, I think I'm not.

At times, therefore, a social worker may have an important role in interpreting the carer's needs to medical, nursing, or care staff. He may also be engaged in helping a 'defeated' family to relinquish their caring role with the minimum of guilt and at the same time helping the elderly person concerned to accept the need for institutional care with the minimum of bitterness, recrimination and depression.

The value of practical help to carers is easier to recognise than is the type of emotional support from which they might benefit. Fuller *et al.* (1979, p. 1684) described how caring relatives seemed to require regular opportunities for discussion:

> Despite maximum support for the caring relative, one of us found such relatives would telephone the hospital from time to time saying they could no longer cope. They were always invited to the unit to discuss their problems, which they did, returning home with the problem unchanged but apparently satisfied and willing to carry on caring for their elderly relatives. Nevertheless, further opportunities to ventilate their feelings were needed.

The authors of this article established regular support groups for relatives caring for a demented elderly person and found that shared experiences in the group were reassuring to relatives; they were also able to express their resentment and anger, to comfort each other during particularly difficult times and to offer advice about the management of care. The benefits of such support groups have been noted also for the relatives of stroke patients who may face not dissimilar problems such as changes in personality, severe physical dependency and fears about the cause of the disabilities, expressed in questions about whether they, the carers, are also likely to have a stroke or become demented.

The kind of support which carers might need in addition to practical services may be to help them understand the processes of ageing, the impact of dependency and in particular the significance of loss of home, of role, of function, or of self-esteem. Equally important, their own response, as carers, to the dependency of their parents may involve such powerful and conflicting feelings that an opportunity to express them is a necessary safety-valve. Caring can be a very lonely, isolating task for all that it is also an expression of love, protection, gratitude and reparation.

In some circumstances the most appropriate form of intervention by the social worker is in working with the elderly person and the carer or family as a group. The concept of social work with families is usually explored in relation to parents rearing children and case examples of family casework and family therapy rarely focus on family interaction which is between an elderly person and his now-adult children, nephews and nieces, or his grandchildren. Yet there are elements in common between the dynamics that are present in a family caring for a young child and those that may be found where an elderly person is receiving care. The elderly person may be scapegoated by the family: marital tension between the adult children or tension between parent and an adolescent child is blamed on the presence of the elderly person. Or, as sometimes happens in families that cannot cope with the rebellion of an adolescent child, the adults reject the offending member. Rather than face the conflict and work out their own problems, the adults find it easier to opt out altogether and request reception into care. Thirdly, the pent-up emotions within the caring family may be expressed in terms not dissimilar to the sentiments expressed by some mothers of young children, as this comment from a social worker shows: 'You speak to the son-in-law or daughter-in-law and they are so tense and frustrated, saying, "If something isn't done, I will end up doing something to her".'

It is, however, inappropriate to pursue the analogy with child-centred family casework too far. One of the basic differences lies in the task being undertaken by the family. With the care of a child the end is eventual independence, whereas with the care of old people the family is having to adjust to increasing dependency and the intimate contact with ageing may present an unwelcome reminder of mortality. The relationships between the old person and his relatives have a long history and whilst it is possible that all involved have grown older and wiser, it is probably more likely that relationship problems have become more entrenched. Attitudes, habits and characteristics which were bearable for short visits or holidays assume greater significance when circumstances demand much closer contact and the adult children may find the sibling rivalries of their childhood unexpectedly reawakened in the context of caring for their elderly parent(s).

It is important to distinguish the different purposes that may be served by working with an elderly person and his family as a group. First, there is the use of family therapy. This is probably of little value if there is a long history of bitterness or emotional coldness in the family or if some of the present tensions appear to be linked with mental illness. In addition, where an elderly person is very confused, very frail, or very deaf, working with the family group is likely to present more difficulties in communication than working with individuals or a much smaller group. Wasser (1966) quotes Milloy who suggests that in certain families one or both of the middle-generation parents may have unresolved problems of separation from their own parents and that these may be activated either at the point where the elderly person becomes extremely dependent or at the time when the adolescent children are seeking to separate from their parents. In both instances, the expression of problems in relation to one or other family member may have a deeper significance and Milloy believes that family therapy including the elderly persons can offer an appropriate form of help.

Secondly, and probably more usually, work with the family as a whole may be associated with decisions as to the future care of the elderly person. Here, the focus is slightly different from interviews which are concerned with the nature of past and present relationships. The social worker (Kirschner, 1979, p. 213):

> [is] not restoring or reconstructing the original family relationships ... [but] assembling the family to deal with the present reality ... Old wounds will not be reopened ... The agenda ... should be a review of the parent's current status and a plan for the future ... [and] the worker should ... guard against regression to previous, inappropriate patterns of behaviour.

Providing this focus is explained and maintained by the social worker, families may meet for such discussions despite previous hostilities and present distress. Thus all, including the elderly person concerned, can participate in the decision-making and the possibility of later recriminations and suspicions can be minimised.

Considerable attention has been paid to the stressful nature of some intergenerational relationships and to the physical and emotional burdens borne by some relatives caring for severely dependent elderly people. Given the at times heroic efforts that are made to avoid institutional care, it is appropriate to stress again the underlying strength of intergenerational bonds which form the backbone of community services to dependent elderly people. Many families, indeed, seem to adjust successfully to the changing circumstances introduced by a severely dependent elderly person – although one should always consider the question 'But at what cost?'. It is important that the needs of the carers do not continue to be overlooked or ignored but are instead studied and explored so that an attempt can be made to help them provide the care that they are willing to offer. Each caregiver and each old person may require a different 'package' of help, depending on individual needs and experiences. As one social worker said, in an attempt to sum up the social work role in supporting old people and their carers: 'You don't always have to put a lot of practical services in. Often the emotional support alone makes the difference.'

Chapter 7

Residential Care of Elderly People

Residential care of elderly people is a subject which has been somewhat neglected by social work practitioners and by writers on social work practice. Most attention to residential care has been focused on the care of children and whilst it is important that the knowledge, principles and practice that have developed in relation to the young are explored in the discussions about the purpose and process of caring for elderly people, there are certain issues which currently are of major significance for residential care of old people.

The first, as might be expected, is a direct consequence of the structure of the elderly population, notably the major increase of the very old in both absolute and proportional terms. The number of people aged 80 to 84 will increase by nearly 31 per cent in the period 1975–2001 and those aged 85 and over by 46 per cent (OPCS, 1978). This means that in 2001 there will be a total of slightly over 1 million in the 80- to 84-year-old group and three-quarters of a million aged 85 and over, which represents an increase of 139,000 and 202,000 respectively over the 1981 figures. The implications for resource provision in the health and the social services are obvious when one remembers that it is the very old who make the greatest demands for a high level of treatment, care and support. Secondly, the past ten years or so have seen a significant increase in domiciliary services and other provision which offers an alternative to long-term residential care. Although the rate of expansion in domiciliary and day care facilities has now been halted or at the very best considerably slowed down, nevertheless, in some authorities at least, it is possible to delay or even prevent admission to permanent care. This, together with the demographic changes, affects who is admitted and at what level of ability. Thirdly, the introduction of a new type of training – the Certificate of Social Service (CSS) – has the potential to influence the pattern of care, the development of residential work and the future relationship between residential and field staff.

These three issues are central to any discussion of residential work with elderly people and, because they are potentially so significant, part of this chapter briefly outlines some of the implications with which field and residential staff alike are concerned.

ATTITUDES TO RESIDENTIAL CARE

In 1977/8, some 128,700 old people in England and Wales were permanently resident in local authority homes for the elderly (CIPFA, 1979). For each of them the decision to move into an institution will have been amongst the most significant that they were required to make during their whole life.

Residential care is rarely considered the preferred means of help or treatment for any client and it is usually accepted as a last resort or is regarded as evidence of failure. This negative opinion of care may well be shared by potential residents, as this comment from a social worker illustrates: 'They are often horrified ... they say "I never thought I'd come to this. You see other people going into a home and you don't think it can happen to you".'

The debate about preferable alternatives to residential care has a long history. Initially it was expressed in terms of the merits of 'outdoor' relief by offering doles to the sick, the aged and the unemployed so that they could remain in their own homes – the alternative being 'indoor' relief which required residence in the workhouse. It is interesting that the image of the workhouse which developed and still persists is one which emphasised the severity of the regime, despite the evidence (Digby, 1978) that in some regions of the country in the nineteenth century, the diet, standard of living and the medical care of the aged or sick residents were considerably superior to those received by their contemporaries outside. Determination to avoid admission to residential care because of its association with the workhouse has remained a powerful underlying motive for many elderly people for delaying or avoiding entry into an elderly persons' home and the survival of some former workhouses as homes or long-term hospitals for elderly patients does little to encourage a more positive view of residential care.

To this historical dimension must be added such factors as the cost of residential care (about one-fifth of total net expenditure by social services departments in England and Wales is on residential care of elderly people) and the by now extensive literature on the unwelcome, the harmful and the occasionally tragic aspects of life in an institution (Goffman, 1961; Townsend, 1962; Robb, 1967; Meacher, 1972). It is the combination of all these factors, rather than any one in isolation, which consigns residential care to its position as a 'residual service' (Payne 1977), a last resort and not a resource with its own particular merits. Whilst this attitude persists, it may direct energy primarily towards avoiding care and not on developing environments and care regimes which would raise the standard of care that is currently offered in many establishments (including long-term hospitals).

Yet as Plank (1977) and others (Sainsbury and Grad, 1971; Sanford, 1975) have demonstrated, the reality of community care is not always so attractive, and the stereotype of institutional care as necessarily 'bad' and community care as necessarily 'good' disregards both the caring functions of residential homes and the shortcomings in domiciliary provision that are experienced by some dependent elderly people living in the community. Moreover, it is important not to underestimate the need that some very frail old people have for care and for security, and the extent to which the daily responsibility for self-care may become a constant source of anxiety. Whilst sheltered housing, group living, intensive domiciliary support and the kind of warning systems outlined in the previous chapter may allow some elderly people to remain in their own homes (or at least give them the choice of whether or not to, which is equally important), there will be some elderly people whose frailty and disability require a level and type of permanent daily care which is currently available only in a residential establishment. Indeed, the certainty of the constant availability of care might be psychologically important for some, especially if they are very old and without close family networks. The recognition that some elderly people may need and indeed wish for residential care turns the community versus institutional care debate into a more positive form, as Brody (1977a, p. 22) points out:

> The issue is not that of institutional care versus community care. The relevant issues are *to identify those for whom long term care is appropriate and to determine the nature of the service and the qualities of the environments that would maximise their well-being.* (italics in original)

RESIDENTIAL CARE – FOR WHOM?

The assessment of an elderly person's 'suitability' for residential care has in recent years become probably more difficult than previously (as is evident, for example, in the debates about whether incontinence should automatically preclude admission to an elderly persons' home) and there is every indication that it is unlikely to become any easier. The wider variety of provisions that may act as alternatives to permanent care, the growing number of frail and disabled elderly people (often without a family) and the present lack of expansion in the residential sector all combine to raise fundamental questions about the purpose of residential care and characteristics of the people whom it is intended to serve.

Recent studies of elderly people accepted as suitable for care have drawn attention to the shortcomings of assessments. The study by Brocklehurst *et al.* (1978) found that of the 100 applicants who had been accepted as requiring residential care and who were then examined by a geriatrician, as many as one-third were considered to require alternative provision such as hospital care, sheltered accommodation, or additional support services in their own homes. From the report of the study it is not clear whether these other provisions had not been considered or whether residential care was being sought as the 'next best' provision because the desired one was unavailable. Either way, however, it is disquieting that apparently inappropriate requests for care are accepted. Marshall and Boaden (1978) also stress the importance of involving the elderly person's general practitioner in the assessment for care; if the inclusion of medical assessment were to become a routine and integral part of the assessment for care, this could uncover incidents of unreported but remediable ill-health and also, if admission does take place, the staff of the home would have accurate information about the elderly person's present state of health and, equally important, precise details about current medication.

The acceptance of apparently 'inappropriate' applications may in part be a consequence of the lack of clarity about the purpose of care mentioned above, although this should not obscure the fact that some at least of the misjudgements seem to arise from practice that falls short of an adequate standard. The development of more precise and thorough assessment procedures is clearly important, given the pressure on beds that currently exists in most local authorities and area health authorities.

Acceptance for care does not, however, always result in admission and it was the factors resulting in admission that formed the subject of a study by Carter and Evans (1978). They followed the 'careers' of elderly people on the waiting list for care in 1973 in one local authority and compared those who were admitted with those who, in 1977, were still alive and still awaiting a vacancy. They found that successful applicants (i.e. those admitted) differed from the unsuccessful not so much in their living circumstances or their level of dependency but in their ability (or the ability of their carers) to *tolerate* their condition. Thus, speedy admission to care was likely to happen if an elderly person living alone reached the point at which he said he could no longer continue as before. His circumstances might not have changed at all but his tolerance of them had. A similar picture was seen in relation to elderly people admitted from within their families: the elderly person's condition often had not altered but either the family was finally defeated by the strain of caring or other factors interfered (such as the arrival of a young baby or the ill-health of the principal carer). The significance of an elderly person's or a family's level of tolerance is yet further evidence of the individuality of each person's coping capacity.

Many homes have some residents who are equally, if not more dependent than patients on long-term geriatric or psychogeriatric wards (Wilkin and Jolley, 1978). In addition, some residents in homes are less dependent than some tenants of sheltered housing or than some people awaiting care (Plank, 1977). This is not necessarily the result of inaccurate assessment and placement, since elderly people's level of dependency may change after admission and such change is not always in one direction: a good standard of physical care may result in a substantial improvement in health, appearance and morale. Unless one is prepared to inflict several moves on elderly residents (those who become more able going to sheltered accommodation, with the possibility of a return to residential care and maybe a move to hospital if and when there is deterioration) it is inevitable that dependency levels in a home will vary. The question is whether the level and type of care in elderly people's homes can be varied to suit individual needs.

For whilst the location of the old person is not necessarily determined by his mental or physical state, his place of residence may crucially affect the type and the level of help available to him. This point was stressed by Wilkin and Jolley (1978) in their study of dependency levels in a group of elderly persons' homes and long-term geriatric and psychogeriatric wards. Their comment (p. 67) is apposite, irrespective of whether the old person is in an institution or being cared for in the community:

> The care, treatment and therapy required by severely impaired old people in institutional care is often very similar whether they happen to be residents in homes, patients in geriatric wards or patients in psychogeriatric wards. The skills of care staff, physiotherapists, doctors, social workers, nurses and occupational therapists are all appropriate to varying degrees, but the availability of any particular service is usually dictated by the institution in which the old person happens to find himself or herself.

Significantly, the authors do not conclude that the answer lies in increasing the number of hospital beds to take the most severely dependent old people. They write (p. 66):

> Evidence from this study relating to successive cohorts of old people in different institutions suggests that many severely impaired people may fare better in mixed residential environments than they do in hospital wards. Rather than changing the balance of provision in favour of hospitals, it may be more effective to increase levels of specialist support for the residential homes, but this would require a much greater element of collaboration within and between agencies than exists at present.

Whether or not residential homes develop as establishments designed and able to provide a wider spectrum of nursing care than is at present the case, there is no doubt that the previous low levels of dependency amongst residents are unlikely to return.

Indeed, with the increase in the very old section of the elderly population and the absence of a corresponding rise in the level of resources available to support and treat them, it is likely that residential homes will be caring for people who are more rather than less frail and disabled. This has many implications, not just, as was mentioned above, for the definition of what 'suitability' for care now means, but also for staffing and for the formulation and practice of a philosophy of care appropriate for a group of elderly residents whose ability to seek satisfaction of their social and emotional needs may be seriously curtailed by physical or mental infirmity.

TRAINING FOR OFFICERS-IN-CHARGE

The training of staff in the residential sector has received far less attention than that accorded to field staff. This is in part a consequence of the low status of residential care as a means of helping clients and, in turn, also contributes to its continued existence as a 'residual service': there are few trained staff to offer adequate supervision to existing workers or to students; the lack of attention to training needs may be seen to imply lack of interest and this may have a detrimental effect on staff morale and recruitment; and the limited opportunities for staff to attend training, compared with greater opportunities available to field staff, may appear as tacit acknowledgement that the residential task requires a low level of skill, or certainly a lower level than fieldwork. There are indications that changes are taking place here, for some local authorities have taken policy decisions to concentrate their training budgets on the residential rather than the fieldwork sector. But it will be a long time before the level of trained staff in residential work comes anywhere near the level in fieldwork and, in terms of CQSW training, for example, the percentage of students completing their training in 1978 and returning to the residential sector was a mere 6·3 per cent, compared with 71·5 per cent who returned to fieldwork (CCETSW, 1978).

Two themes have formed an important part of the approach to training for residential care. The first is uncertainty about the nature and the extent of genericism in residential care: is there a body of knowledge and practice skills which is transferrable across client groups and across different types of establishment? The Williams Committee (1967) made a major statement on this issue when it recommended that there should be separate training courses for residential workers which would equip them for a wide range of residential settings. The second theme is the debate about the extent to which residential care is, or should be, a social work activity. The working party on training for residential work established by the Central Council for Education and Training in Social Work expressed its conclusion in the title of its report (CCETSW Paper No. 3, 1973) – *Residential Work is a Part of Social Work* – and it proposed a unified training for field and residential staff. The influence of the unitary approach to social work has given further impetus to the inclusion of residential care within the mainstream of social work (Payne, 1977) and more recently, the Jay Committee (1979), which reported on the care of mentally handicapped people, concluded that the principles, knowledge base and skills required to 'normalise' the lives of mentally handicapped people are essentially those that are located within a social work framework.

Like the long-term care of mentally handicapped people, care of the elderly has retained much of its nursing origins although it has developed within the local authority to a far greater extent than residential care of those who are mentally handicapped. Nursing staff have traditionally occupied the senior posts in elderly persons' homes and there are still establishments where nursing uniform is worn by 'matron' and her deputy. By contrast, the care staff are classed as manual workers. Whatever the original reasons for this designation, the low status accorded to the direct caring activities gives little acknowledgement to the level of sensitivity and interpersonal skills which are required of care staff if residential care is not to demean the residents experiencing it.

However, at a time when the place of residential care within social work is becoming more widely accepted, it is arguable in respect of elderly persons' homes that the increasing level of frailty of the residents makes the presence of staff with a nursing qualification more necessary than it was when people were admitted at a younger age and with fewer problems associated with infirmity. Evidence from a small-scale study in one local authority points to the need for residential staff to improve their ability to detect the onset of deafness and of failing sight and the early signs of minor, remediable disorders (Roe and Guillem, 1978). It may be, therefore, that staff with a nursing qualification should develop a more clearly defined health-screening role as part of their work. But to accept the importance of the nursing contribution to direct care and to preventive health care is not necessarily to suggest that a nursing qualification is the most appropriate one for the head of a home.

Many of the discussions about qualifications for heads of homes have focused on the nursing or social work debate, reflecting the contribution of nursing to the direct care of those who are unable, by reason of infirmity, handicap, or babyhood, to care for themselves. In respect of training for the residential care of elderly people, however, it is arguable that an occupational therapy qualification could be equally appropriate, as is evidenced by those OTs who manage day centres for physically handicapped people or who have effectively influenced the regime in some geriatric wards so that elderly patients are encouraged to assume greater responsibility for self-care and for the general environment of the ward.

But even if one accepts the current opinion that training for heads of homes should be provided from a social work perspective, the question of appropriate training still remains unclear. Two options exist: CQSW or CSS training, and it is important to bear in mind that the training available to other staff in the home may well depend on that which is appropriate for the person in charge. CCETSW (1975, pp. 6–7) has defined two groups of staff for whom a CSS course is intended:

> the first includes those who require some of the knowledge and skills which have been developed within the social work profession, combined with substantial knowledge and skills needed by some of the senior staff in residential and day care establishments … The second broad category includes those assistant staff in residential, field, community, domiciliary and day services, who carry substantial responsibility in relation to clients but are not charged with the overall responsibility for them …

It is beyond the scope of this book to argue the pros and cons of CSS training and it is in any case probably too early to see how it will take effect. But already two trends are becoming apparent.

The first is that Cypher's (1977) prediction that the CSS could become the accepted qualification for work with elderly people is showing early signs of fulfilment. By far the most commonly chosen 'main client group' for study is the elderly; 37·4 per cent of the CSS students in 1978 opted for this client group, more than double the second-highest client group, chosen by 14·6 per cent of the students. Secondly, in the same year, 57·3 per cent of the students were from the residential sector whereas the figures on CQSW students show that only 6·3 per cent of them went into residential work (CCETSW, 1978). These figures raise serious questions. On what basis does a small proportion of residential staff receive CQSW training whereas the majority are receiving a different type of training on CSS courses? In which homes are these few CQSW staff located? Unfortunately the figures do not state to which level of post students return or to which establishments. This is important, given that it is as yet unclear either whether the CQSW or the CSS is the most appropriate training for the post of officer-in-charge or, indeed, whether this depends on the establishment concerned.

The major problem is that in residential care in general and in care of old people in particular, there has been a lack of clarification about the social work role, and CSS training is taking place despite current inadequacy of conceptualisation of both social work and social service tasks. It would be most unfortunate if, in the context of this uncertainty, patterns of training for certain client groups and, equally important, for certain settings in which social work is practised become established before respective roles and tasks have been clarified.

An additional factor must also be considered here. The earlier statements (Birch, 1976; BASW, 1977a) about the tasks which should appropriately be undertaken by CQSW staff have recently been incorporated in the pay settlements which followed the social work strike in 1979. These are local settlements and so there is a degree of variation between authorities but the grading of social work staff into levels one, two and three according to training and experience is based in part on the amount of supervision which they should receive and also on the tasks they undertake. Thus, in some authorities, activities which involve loss of liberty for the client or permanent change of home are considered appropriate only for level two and, in some cases, only for level three workers. Exactly where and how CSS staff should be incorporated into this grading system is as yet unclear, but at least two outcomes are possible. To begin with, very little change in respect of work with elderly people might follow, and CSS workers would continue to take major responsibility for this client group; if this is the case it will be interesting to see how far CSS workers who have taken 'children' or 'families' as their main client group will be able to assume the same range of tasks as their colleagues undertake with elderly clients, thereby involving them with receptions into care and other tasks normally accepted as requiring a CQSW worker.

The second possibility is that if, following grading systems, CQSW staff become more involved in, for example, admissions to elderly persons' homes, then the relationship between field and residential work could be seriously affected if the officer-in-charge does not hold a comparable qualification. It could mean that the fieldworker on the appropriate grade for such work would retain total or at least the greater part of responsibility both for assessment and for the way the admission is managed. This would seem a retrograde step, given the benefits for staff and clients alike of demolishing the long-existing barrier between residential work and fieldwork and of developing ways in which there might be shared and flexible modes of working which were not dictated by setting.

It is evident from the preceding paragraphs that there is much need for examination and discussion of current developments in training for residential work; the issues are extremely complex and the repercussions for future practice are significant. Alongside the debates about training for officers-in-charge, there is the important subject of training for care staff which in its own right raises questions about the practicable, as well as the desirable, type of training they should receive. This in turn has implications for their conditions of employment, given their current status as manual workers.

ASPECTS OF PRACTICE

1 *Admission to care*

There are some elderly people who are very lonely or who are anxious about their capacity to survive on their own who may find the prospect of care a relief, even if it is tinged with regrets that they can no longer enjoy their former independence. But for others the image of the workhouse, the understandable reluctance to leave familiar surroundings for a strange environment and the inescapable significance of the need for that level of care all contribute to a predominantly negative and possibly fearful view of care. An additional difficulty for the client may be the lack of information that is available to help him or her reach a decision; this applies on both the factual level of what the proposed home is like and also on the experiential level, since, for most people, 'going into a home' has few, if any, parallels to events earlier in life.

Anxious or bewildered clients may place considerable pressure on the worker to assume responsibility for decisions that have to be made: 'Well, what do *you* advise?'; 'Do you think I'd be happy in that home?'; or, in tones of resignation or finality, 'I'll do whatever you think is best'. Elderly people whose need for care has arisen suddenly – perhaps after a stroke which has severely affected their capacity to look after themselves – may have had little prior need to consider the possibility of residential care and thus are faced with the decision at a time when other adjustments must also be made. Yet those whose vulnerability is sufficiently high to necessitate admission may also be the most vulnerable to the experience of being admitted; Brody (1977a) cites the research studies which identify that elderly people who are physically ill, who are depressed or confused, or who are moved against their will are the most likely to suffer adversely from the transfer to institutional care.

For the relatives of applicants or of residents, there are likely to be equally strong feelings of sadness, of anxiety about the kind of care to be provided, and guilt that they are not fulfilling the caring obligations of the family. Residential care may indeed be less easy for many relatives to accept than is provision of hospital care, since the latter implies a need for medical care (which a layman cannot be expected to provide) whereas it might be thought that any caring person could fulfil the 'looking after' task undertaken in residential homes. If contact between the old person and his relatives is to be maintained after admission, it is important that the feelings on both sides are explored and worked with.

Admission to care may be viewed as an on-going process in

which certain tasks will be faced. In a useful article, Pope (1978) identifies four phases in this process: *preparation*, which lasts from the point of making an application to notification of a place; *separation*, which is the period from notification to the moment of admission; *transition*, which is the first day in the home; and *incorporation*, which is the period from the end of that first day to the time when the resident feels 'at home'. It is significant that 'transition' is the only part of this process which has an identifiable and predictable time-limit; some applicants will spend several years in phase one and some will be expected to experience the phase of separation in a matter of days, for example, in those local authorities where vacancies must be filled within a week or so of client and worker being informed. How to cope with the unpredictability of timing and to use the time appropriately has yet to be fully explored.

Pope's first phase of preparation could perhaps be extended to include the process by which the applicant (or the person applying on the applicant's behalf) comes to make the decision that care is desirable or unavoidable. Tobin and Lieberman (1976) have found evidence that many of the feelings of abandonment, rejection and hopelessness for the future which can be found amongst the residents of old people's homes are also expressed by people who are on the waiting list for care. This suggests that it is an oversimplification to attribute the flattened affect of many residents to the care regime they experience or to their location in an institution. There are implications here for the way in which care might be provided, for, again, as with other aspects of caring for elderly people, the importance of restoring self-respect and of re-establishing patterns of communication and of self-expression are vital. If residents come into care with existing deprivations, this suggests that care programmes or care regimes should develop in such a way as to restore and promote self-esteem in addition to the provision of physical care. Compensation for deprivation is more commonly discussed in relation to the young – compensatory education, for example – but there is a need to explore the concept of a 'compensatory environment' in the care of elderly people.

The difficulties of managing the preparation period which were mentioned above are evident in the following quotation from a social worker. She believed that, whenever possible, her clients should not make an application for care unless they had seen what a residential home was like, so a preliminary visit to a home formed part of her work in the preparation period:

> You go to the home with the elderly person who is given a very nice welcome and a cup of tea in a sitting room and she can talk with the other residents. If *they* say 'I've been very comfortable here', they'll sell the home for you – and then of course you have to say, 'Well, I'm sorry you can't move in next week, there's a waiting list you see'.

For any elderly person, a move into residential care is likely to involve practical planning about distribution of property and the items to be taken to the home as well as psychological preparation for a new environment (Brody, 1977a; Yawney and Slover, 1973). Decisions and adjustments such as these may well need to be worked out over time so that the people concerned can participate and feel that they have retained some control over what is happening rather than being turned into objects of hasty and bewildering plans.

In some local authorities, it has been possible for homes to become identified with a discrete geographical area. This increases the likelihood that new residents will have acquaintances already in the home or that they will at least share a common knowledge about the locality and how it has developed and changed. There are potential advantages, too, for field and residential staff who have the opportunity to work together in this pre-admission period. An officer-in-charge from a home which had a strong neighbourhood identity described the benefits from her perspective of being involved in assessments and pre-admission work:

> I ask them 'Have you ever seen [the home]?' and I'll invite them to come for the day or for a short holiday. I don't like admitting for permanent care straight away – it can raise a lot of resentment, 'You brought me here' sort of thing, and we will then bear the brunt of that. And then maybe I'll visit them two or three times in their own homes …

This link with residents *before* they are admitted is of value for several reasons. It helps care staff to see the new resident as a person with an identity who lived in a particular house in a certain street. This knowledge can provide the subject for conversation and can also help care staff to find ways of fostering the links between the past environment and the present one. Many residents will have few surviving friends or relatives who have known or even seen them outside an institution; this problem is also found in relation to children in long-term care, whose 'pre-care' identity and experiences have become hazy or forgotten because there is no one around who shares them. Visiting elderly people before admission is one way in which care staff can ensure that a resident's past life is not cut off by admission.

Emergency admissions or admissions straight from hospital following only partial recovery from an illness, fall or a stroke pose particular problems in preparation in that the phases of preparation and of separation become 'telescoped'. An elderly hospital patient may be admitted to the first home to have a vacancy, and thus be unable to prepare for admission to a known environment; this was a matter of concern to a social worker who was interviewed:

> This is something that bothers me. Take my client – she's nowhere to picture where she might be discharged to. She hasn't got a picture of 'home' now, she hasn't a vision of what 'home' might be like ...

Moreover, discharge to care rather than to one's own home may seem like failure, coming at the end of an unsuccessful struggle to achieve former levels of function. In such circumstances, the 'separation' stage assumes particular importance and rushing through the admission in the space of a couple of days in order neither to 'lose' the vacancy nor to 'block' the hospital bed may be especially damaging to the elderly person concerned. For preparation time is thought to be an important influence on the elderly person's adjustment to care. There is evidence (Gutman and Herbert, 1977) that plentiful information about the move and careful planning with the elderly person about how it is to be accomplished can enable quite impaired elderly people to experience relocation without adverse effects of increased confusion or increased mortality rate.

For those workers who are with old people during the actual admission, there is no avoiding the inevitable sadness of the event, however well preparations have been made and however much the old person may be deceptively muted. As a social worker pointed out: 'Old people are very good at covering up their feelings ... they might go very quiet, but they'll have a stiff upper lip ...' There is much for the new resident to take in, however well prepared he or she has been. In the following quotation an officer-in-charge describes the importance of allowing time for reflection and her reference to 'special relationships' is evocative of good basic practice in residential work with children:

> Never overwhelm them when they arrive with 'This is Mrs X and that's Mr Y' – don't overwhelm them. It's a very sensitive time. They don't want people rushing up with 'Would you like to do this or that?' They might want to sit and think about what's happening. You may see them sitting a bit withdrawn – let them, they're not going to be over the moon at coming to Part III. They need to think about it – the loss of privacy, loss of independence, loneliness. But I will introduce them to their own care attendant – the care attendants each have so many residents to look after. It's important for staff and residents to have special relationships.

Brody (1977a) emphasises the importance of not abandoning the new resident on admission day. She argues that relatives or a close friend should be encouraged to stay with the elderly person for some time, helping him to unpack, arrange his personal belongings and locate important parts of the establishment such as the lavatory and dining room. However often the new resident has visited the home beforehand, he is unlikely to have been able to explore the building in relation to what is now his room and orientation to new surroundings will therefore be important. Brody believes that the social worker who has undertaken the admission should also participate in this first day, as part of the means by which transfer is effected from one environment to another. If residential and field staff can work together and share this time which is very important for the elderly person, such practice should lessen the likelihood of the elderly person feeling that he has been 'handed on' and the residential staff that they have been 'landed with' a new resident.

2 *After admission*

Like the phase of preparation, Pope's fourth phase –

incorporation – has no predictable time-limit. Yawney and Slover (1973, p. 88) quote American studies which indicated that 'most elderly residents never completely accept their new world' and this is perhaps to be expected given the extensive changes that life in a residential setting so often requires (Consumer's Viewpoint, *Social Work Today*, 1978). There has been considerable controversy over the extent of the negative effects of admission to care. Some studies (Aldrich and Mendkoff, 1963; Miller and Lieberman, 1965) have shown that the relocation is associated with onset or increase in confusion, a decline in physical health and early mortality. More recently, this pessimistic view has been challenged by Gutman and Herbert (1977) who, as mentioned above, found that plentiful information about the impending move and careful planning with the elderly person concerned can enable quite impaired people to experience relocation without adverse effects. Borup *et al.* (1979), reviewing the available American literature on the relocation of elderly people, came to the firm conclusion that there is insufficient proof that a negative response to the process is widespread and the work of Pattie and Gilleard (1978) in this country supports that view.

Nevertheless, whilst some new residents may appear to benefit or at least to suffer no ill-effects from admission, there is little doubt that the post-admission period is a critical one where it is not unusual for new residents to exhibit disturbances of mood, orientation and sleep patterns. Brearley (1977) has emphasised the dislocation to established patterns of living and of relationships caused by entering care and the need to learn new patterns of relating to family, friends, care staff and fellow residents. For some elderly persons this may be a confusing time, when they are partway between relinquishing one style of living and establishing another one. The so-called 'settling down' or 'settling in' period is one characterised by relearning; indeed, the term 'working through' might provide a more accurate picture of what is required both of the resident and of the people close to him. Kiley (1977) views the major contribution of the social worker as coming within the post-admission period. As the section on loss in a previous chapter indicated, there is considerable evidence to show that adjustment to dramatic change involves coping with powerful feelings and this requires a stamina which frail elderly people may well not possess. It is important to bear in mind that even when an elderly person has wanted the security and the comfort of residential care, this period of adjustment is still experienced and some degree of doubt or sadness is likely to be felt. An officer-in-charge described how the significance of the move may take a few weeks to be realised:

> One lady, she had a smile on her face and made herself right at home when she was admitted. But it was early days; it's all right to do that for a week or two ... But I always say 'Wait for the crunch'. Once it's hit you that you've closed your front door, you're in here now and you look around and what have you got? – One and a half drawers, half a wardrobe and a bed in a four-bedded room and you're ninety-four. How much have we progressed, how much *are* we doing for the elderly?

In this adjustment period the admitting social worker has an important role in helping the elderly person to transfer into the life of the home. Trust in the care staff and in the other residents will develop slowly (if it develops at all) and only when it has been established should the admitting social worker consider reducing contact. Moreover, it is likely that if a new resident is worried or unhappy he will confide in 'his' social worker rather than in a member of the care staff who is seen as being 'for' the home. This is partly because the admitting social worker is in contact with the resident's past life but also because of the difficulty that dependent people of any age have in questioning the care they are receiving; such behaviour seems ungrateful or churlish and there is always the fear (which may or may not be unfounded) that reprisals might follow.

Just as the elderly person has to adjust to admission, so do his friends, relatives and significant acquaintances. Visiting people in institutions of any kind is often a difficult and embarrassing task, even more so if communication is constrained by guilt or reproach, and the admitting social worker may need to facilitate regular visiting patterns. Our understanding of the dynamics of visits by parents to their child in care should be applied to visits by adult children to their elderly parent: the rejection that might initially be shown towards the visitor; the absence of overt gratitude at receiving a visit; the tension that can arise between care staff and the visitor; and the showering of gifts upon the one who is in care. It is a myth that visits are always joyful occasions and care staff, the elderly resident and visiting relatives may need to consider how best they can each cope with the experience of receiving and making visits. This may be on a deceptively simple level of finding ways of making contact. Brody (1977a) suggests that the strained atmosphere of many visits can be diminished if the visitor and the resident share a mutual interest – the family photograph album could be brought, for example, or a magazine which both could look at, or a game of cards or dominoes could be played. These 'aids' to managing visits are simple once thought about, but relatives or friends (who are also learning a new pattern of behaviour) may feel inhibited or uncertain about what is permissible. This uncertainty and awkwardness may in turn lead to visits that are unhappy for all involved and future contacts may always be clouded by these initial somewhat fraught experiences.

This involvement by the social worker in the post-admission stage can, therefore, be seen as both preventive and promotional, supporting the various parties concerned through relocation and establishing the foundation of relationships in the new environment. The social worker does not wait until problems are referred but assumes an active role, initiating contact and discussion with the aim of preventing difficulties from occurring.

Several accounts exist of relatives' groups, led by social workers who aimed thereby to encourage and facilitate visiting by relatives. Nolen and Schaengold (1978) commented on the common concerns of many relatives. Is their elderly parent or aunt receiving the right kind of care? Are the staff sensitive to the old person's likes and dislikes? How can they communicate with their elderly relative who is becoming confused and unable to hold a normal conversation? How should they cope with family bereavements? The experiences of Streltzer (1979) indicate that grandchildren too may benefit from attending a short-term group, especially shortly after their grandparents' admission when they are also learning how to establish visiting patterns at a time when feelings about the admission and the way it was handled may still be confused.

It seems that if contact between residents and their families is to be maintained over time, a positive attempt must be made to keep contact alive. The longer an elderly person is in a home, the less likely it is that he will receive visitors; and mentally infirm residents are also less likely than those who are lucid to be visited (Wilkin and Jolley, 1978). Although it is inevitable that some of the older residents will have outlived their close family, this falling-away of visitors has been noted in relation to children in long-term care, for example, and it takes little imagination to see that it is not easy to make regular visits to someone who is becoming increasingly infirm or who, like some children in care, may find it difficult to understand and accept why visiting relatives do not offer permanent care.

To conclude this chapter, it is important to consider the social work contribution to the regime of the home. Brody (1977a) recommends that in each long-term care establishment, there should be at least one full-time social worker to each fifty or sixty residents, engaged, as appropriate, in individual work with residents and their relatives, group work with residents, relatives, or staff and consultation and support for staff members. Brody argues that this worker should be there not in a management capacity nor as head of home but on account of skills in direct work. Whether or not this social work role can, in Britain, be part of the role of the officer-in-charge is as yet unclear, partly because the contribution of social work to long-term care is so little developed.

There are, however, several areas where the involvement of a social worker as an integral part of the care team seems particularly appropriate. The presence of a social worker in the home is not meant to imply that all residents routinely require social work help by virtue of being residents. Some may have no need of help on an individual basis, once it is clear that they have become 'incorporated' in the home. Some, however, may experience problems of adjustment over a long period and in these circumstances it may be appropriate for the social worker in the home gradually to assume a more significant role with the resident and for the admitting social worker gradually to withdraw. Such transfers would, or course, have to be planned carefully and sensitively and would probably be preceded by a period where the admitting social worker and the social worker in the home worked jointly with the resident.

Residents may at times benefit from participating in a planned series of groups which deal with shared problems: newly admitted residents, for example, who face a common task of adjustment; socially very deprived people; residents who have had a stroke; even disoriented people, who may be encouraged to share their memories even if their grasp of the present is tenuous. Simply sharing the experience of growing old and being old may help residents who are coping with this changed status (Harris, 1979). Or the relatives' groups described earlier might be organised by a social work practitioner in the home.

In considering the contribution that the social worker might make to the overall pattern of routine care in the residential home, it is interesting to see the kind of contribution that social workers are making to the care of patients in units for young people who are chronically sick and disabled. Here the social worker has become involved in the quality of life and the quality of social care (DHSS, 1978, p. 285):

> I am there as a team member to develop the residents' potential but as a *social worker* to make sure that there is social welfare in its broadest context. [This will include] my asking 'Why isn't Marion wearing teeth?'. 'Oh, because she is an epileptic and she might swallow them.' – 'Well, I think she would look prettier with teeth.' (italics in original)

Mercer and Kane (1979) draw attention to the 'learned helplessness' that is to be found amongst residents in long-term care who submit to the routine of the home and no longer carry out the everyday household tasks such as making their bed or dusting which, prior to admission, they had been able to perform. Mercer and Kane's small-scale study suggests that this helplessness is associated with the feelings of hopelessness that may be found in long-term care establishments and that to increase residents' control over their lives has the effect of raising their morale. The authors emphasise the creative, promotional role which social workers might adopt (p. 109):

> Social workers can help develop programs and policies within homes that will increase the degree of control, choice and predictability available to residents. In addition, it seems important that such programs are contingent on an individualized assessment of the residents of the home to insure that the control and choice being offered correspond to what the residents themselves value ... With their professional penchant for individualization, social workers would do well to expend their energy in determining what is

important to each individual rather than focusing exclusively on the residents' problems.

That such work may take the form of apparently minor innovations is illustrated by Mercer and Kane's study which demonstrated that positive results could come simply from involving residents in the selection and care of indoor plants. Of crucial importance, however, was the fact that the residents were not simply given a plant but were encouraged to take the opportunity of selecting a plant and were later involved in taking cuttings, repotting, and so on. In this way, the plant became a vehicle for conversations and shared activities both between residents and between staff and residents. The residents in the home came from a rural area and most of them had been directly involved with horticulture and agriculture throughout their lives; hence the deliberate choice by Mercer and Kane of an activity which would evoke memories of past experiences. For residents in an urban community or for those who are members of particular ethnic or religious groups, there are likely to be other activities which may form the focus of work.

Examples of elderly persons' homes in Britain where residents have been encouraged to become involved in how the home is run are few and far between and homes that change their regime in this way are still very much pioneers in this work (Maiston and Gupta, 1977). The process by which such changes may be made possible is not yet fully explored – for example, the support and consultation that residential staff may require in order to feel confident to initiate change and the way in which residents may be enabled to influence any changes that are proposed. Whilst the current levels of inactivity and apathy that characterise so many lounges in elderly persons' homes may be demoralising for staff and for residents, it is equally important that change and activity is not inflicted on residents who have, literally, to live with the consequences of change.

Conclusion

This book has attempted to illustrate the complexity and diversity of the needs and circumstances of elderly people. It is therefore a cause for concern that many social workers, even after training, fail to individualise the needs of elderly people, seeing them, rather, as a homogeneous group – 'The Elderly' – whose problems are of a practical nature which can be approached according to routine and straightforward procedures. This raises serious questions about the way in which social workers have been taught. Is it because social work teachers have concentrated their teaching too narrowly – in that work with clients at risk focuses on child abuse, that the concept of self-determination is explored only in relation to adolescents or to adults on probation, or that examples of the practice of crisis intervention or task-centred work come from the field of work with young families? Similar questions may be asked of staff from other disciplines who teach social work students. Does the sociology of the family focus on the nuclear rather than the three- or four-generation family? Are concepts of role and status explored in relation to the old as well as the young? Does teaching on human growth and development largely exclude the psychology of ageing? Are learning and cognition discussed in relation both to children and old people? It is important that teaching about ageing and the problems of elderly people is integrated into all parts of social work education – into what might be termed the 'core' of the course. Otherwise the notion that social work training and practice is not 'about' old people is likely to be perpetuated.

Part of the content of this generic teaching may lie in helping students apply what they learn in respect of one problem or client group to other clients and problems. For example, to consider how understanding of receiving a child into care may help them with other receptions into care: of a mentally handicapped boy into a hostel, for example, an elderly person into a residential home, a young man into prison. Parsloe (in DHSS, 1978, p. 335) suggests that social work teachers, as a group, 'have largely failed to develop concepts which liberate ideas from the prison of a particular client group and facilitate their transfer to others'. Students may need help with the difficult intellectual task of making such links; it is certainly something too important to be left to chance.

Nor can the system of offering 'electives' or 'options' be more than a partial means of informing students about certain aspects of social work. The fact that options often focus on a particular client group or problem may, indeed, reinforce the tendency to compartmentalise knowledge and, in addition, students who attend options are usually 'the converted' who already have an interest in the subject. This is particularly significant when options are offered on the less popular aspects of social work.

It would, however, be misleading to imply that sole responsibility lies with social work education. Within many social services departments there have been few attempts to develop a system of priorities which improves upon the crude reliance on client group as the main determinant of work allocation. Even where social work assistants have job descriptions which emphasise that they should assist social workers and not carry their own cases, an informal practice has often arisen whereby they have acquired and indeed at times sought an autonomous caseload (DHSS, 1978). In addition, few team leaders have received much help in learning how to offer generic supervision and they may, therefore, be ill-equipped to provide a stimulating learning experience for team members who might be motivated to work with elderly clients. Thus the stereotypes of routine, straightforward work are confirmed.

In some departments an attempt has been made to improve the standards of service to elderly and handicapped clients by the creation of teams which work only with these clients. These teams may contain both social work staff and also assistants, home help organisers, OTs, technical officers for the blind and so on. Thus they offer the opportunity for greater sharing between social work and social service staff which may be particularly important for elderly and disabled clients. There are, however, several points to be considered. First, as has been seen in relation to the intake/long-term division found in some offices, the establishment of one special team is likely to restrict the focus of work of the others; 'hiving off' one client group in this way allows and indeed encourages other workers to withdraw completely from work with elderly people. Given that such work is often already on the periphery of mainstream social work and, it could be argued, needs to be integrated rather than segregated, it is possible that separate teams for elderly clients might encourage the view that old people require a totally different kind of help. Moreover, there is the danger that because of their focus on a client group currently afforded low status, such teams may be susceptible to being viewed as 'second-class' teams requiring a lower level of skill or enjoying less prestige than teams specialising with other client groups.

On the other hand, the presence of teams committed to the cause, as it were, could do much to advance knowledge about work with elderly clients – especially if they were able to provide stimulating placements for students. (A major difficulty in encouraging students' interest in work with elderly clients arises from the absence of fieldwork supervisors who could offer such experience.) Possibilities of experimentation, of case-sharing between different workers and of forging closer links with residential staff and with primary health care teams increase if a small group of people can devote their time and energy to such tasks. But it would be unrealistic to see in specialist teams 'the answer' to serving the needs of elderly people, especially if fundamental attitudes within the social work profession as a whole remain unchallenged and unchanged. The concept of specialisation post-Seebohm is too complex to allow such easy answers and whilst a specialist team for elderly clients may be an important *administrative* means of ensuring that elderly clients are given priority by at least some staff this should not be confused with other definitions of 'specialist' which imply that work is 'different' or 'more advanced' (Vickery, 1973).

This book has, of necessity, been selective in the subjects which were included and some chapters, notably the one on residential care, require more detailed attention than has been possible here.

The focus has mainly been on the interaction between worker and a named client, which reflects the author's concern to encourage social workers to be more aware of what they do, how they interact with clients and the knowledge and skill which they use, sometimes unconsciously.

But, to an extent, the content of the book has been shaped by the available literature. There are major gaps in available knowledge – for example, there is little information about what actually happens in residential homes, between residents, between staff and residents and between the staff. How do they all relate to each other? What do they talk about and when? The literature on group work is heavily biased towards groups in psychiatric hospitals or day centres, intermediate treatment, adolescents and young adults. It would be instructive to see more accounts of the application of group-work theory and practice to elderly people who are in long-term care, attending day centres, or in community groups. Similarly, in the community work literature, there are few accounts of community action in those deprived inner city areas where mobile and better-off residents have moved out, leaving behind those who are sick, disabled, elderly, or poor; the emphasis in the case studies of work in inner city areas is usually on the young. The absence of literature relating practice to elderly people may itself contribute to current negative attitudes about the potential for social work with elderly people.

However, at the time this book was going to press, there appeared several interesting additions to the literature on old age and on the role of the social worker. It was too late to include them in the main body of the text but they are sufficiently important to be mentioned here. The first is a discussion document on civil liberty in old age (Norman, 1980) and it is to be hoped that this will stimulate and inform discussion amongst all people who are involved with the care of old people and concerned about the balance between rights and risks.

Secondly, two articles were published which demonstrate the potential for social workers to work with and through other people. In an account of her role with a group of nurses caring for elderly women on a long-term ward of a psychiatric hospital, Coulshed (1980) describes how she introduced nursing staff to the techniques of Reality Orientation, in an attempt to help the nurses improve their methods of relating to these isolated and often confused patients. Coulshed had adopted this approach, rather than working individually with a few patients, because she was aware that many of the problems in the ward (low staff morale and withdrawn, institutionalised patients, for example) were related to the regime in the ward and the absence of meaningful relationships between staff and patients. The article reports the effectiveness of her work with the staff group.

Challis and Davies (1980) provide a more detailed account of the Kent Community Care Project which was described above in Chapter 5. In their article they draw together the findings of earlier interim reports of the project and they present a picture of social workers as the managers of a domiciliary care system aimed at meeting the needs of the most vulnerable elderly people in the community. They describe the activities involved as follows (p. 10): 'Firstly, a close assessment of client need; secondly, choosing amongst alternative ways of providing care; thirdly providing the necessary degree of psychological understanding that should suffuse such a care system ...' Success can be judged from the adequacy and stability of the arrangements that are made for care and Challis and Davies conclude: 'The responsibility demanded by this kind of activity cannot be relegated to the level of routine procedures ... and furthermore is surely more satisfying to practitioners as a result of being stimulating, demanding and more effective for clients.'

Research currently being undertaken by the National Institute for Social Work should add to our understanding of the social work role in the formation and the support of caring networks in the community. To date, social work has not been active in such work, but the influence of the unitary approach (see, for example, Pincus and Minahan, 1973) and the mounting needs of frail elderly people in the community must surely provide the impetus for developing this aspect of work.

There seems little doubt, particularly at a time of retrenchment rather than expansion, that elderly people and the management of care will continue to be very low priority for social work help unless significant changes take place in the way that social work and social service is practised. Elsewhere there is evidence of the reluctance of social workers to transfer clients who no longer need social work help, and the apparent unwillingness of social workers to ascribe certain tasks to volunteers or ancillary staff whilst retaining the main responsibility for the case (Goldberg and Fruin, 1976; Holme and Maizels, 1978). Other studies (Goldberg *et al.*, 1978; DHSS, 1978) have suggested that social workers are spending time on tasks which could as well be undertaken by someone without their type of training: for example, offering advice, advocacy and information on welfare rights, housing and financial problems; providing transport for clients when this is not an intrinsic part of the social work treatment; collecting and delivering aids. In many departments there appears to have been little attempt to deploy non-social work staff in roles which could relieve qualified staff of some routine tasks. Equally, however, social workers are often reluctant to define their task more narrowly or to see their work as one activity which is a discrete specialist part of a wider 'package' of intervention which may be offered by social services departments. The implications of social work having a narrower range of tasks but spread over a wide range of clients are considerable – for teachers, practitioners, managers and social service staff alike. Yet if social work is to be offered on an equitable basis to all clients who require that type of help, it is important that such changes in the organisation of work take place, alongside the changes in outlook, attitudes and practice suggested in this book.

References

Abrams, M. (1978a), *Beyond Three Score and Ten: A First Report on a Survey of the Elderly* (Mitcham: Age Concern Publications).

Abrams, M. (1978b), report of a seminar on the OPCS survey 'The elderly at home', held 17 March (London: DHSS).

Abrams, P. (1977), 'Community care: some research problems and priorities', *Policy and Politics*, vol. 6, no. 2 (December), pp. 125–51.

Age Concern (1974), *Housing and Related Benefits* (Mitcham: Age Concern Publications).

Aldrich, C. K., and Mendkoff, E. (1963) 'Relocation of the aged and disabled: a mortality study', *Journal of the American Geriatrics Society*, vol. 11, pp. 185–94.

Anderson, F. (1973), 'Health needs of the elderly', in Canvin, R. W., and Pearson, N. G. (eds), *Needs of the Elderly for Health and Welfare Services*, pp. 27–31.

Anderson, F. (1977), 'The role of the physician', in Exton-Smith, A. N., and Evans, J. G. (eds), *Care of the Elderly*, pp. 169–75.

Anonymous poem (1977) 'The eighth age of woman', *Community Care*, no. 178, p. 22.

Arie, T. (1973), 'Psychiatric needs of the elderly', in Canvin, R. W., and Pearson, N. G. (eds), *Needs of the Elderly for Health and Welfare Services*, pp. 37–45.

Arie, T. (1977), 'Issues in the psychiatric care of the elderly', in Exton-Smith, A. N., and Evans, J. G., *Care of the Elderly*, pp. 67–80.

Avon Social Services Department (1977), *Multiple Use of Services by the Elderly* (Bristol: Avon Social Services Department).

Biestek, F. P. (1961), *The Casework Relationship* (London: Allen & Unwin).

Birch Report (1976), *Manpower and Training for the Social Services – Report of the Working Party* (London: HMSO).

Blenkner, M. (1965), 'Social work and family relationships in later life with some thoughts on filial maturity', in Shanas, E., and Streib, G. (eds), *Social Structure and the Family* (Englewood Cliffs, NJ: Prentice-Hall).

Blenkner, M., Bloom, M., and Neilsen, M. (1971), 'A research and demonstration project of protective services', *Social Casework*, vol. 52, no. 8, pp. 483–99.

Borup, J. H., Gallego, D. T., and Heffernan, P. G. (1979), 'Relocation and its effects on mortality', *Gerontologist*, vol. 19, no. 2 (April), pp. 135–40.

Bosanquet, N. (1978), *A Future for Old Age* (London: Temple Smith/New Society).

Brearley, C. P. (1975), *Social Work, Ageing and Society* (London: Routledge & Kegan Paul).

Brearley, C. P. (1977), *Residential Work with the Elderly* (London: Routledge & Kegan Paul).

British Association of Social Workers (BASW) (1977a), *The Social Work Task*, BASW Working Party Report (London: BASW).

British Association of Social Workers (1977b), 'Guidelines for social work with the elderly', *Social Work Today*, vol. 8, no. 27 (12 April), pp. 7–15.

Brocklehurst, J. C., Carty, M. H., Leeming, J. T., and Robinson, J. M. (1978), 'Medical screening of old people accepted for residential care', *Lancet* (15 July), pp. 141–3.

Brody, E. M. (1977a), *Long Term Care of Older People* (New York: Human Sciences Press).

Brody, E. M. (1977b), 'Environmental factors in dependency', in Exton-Smith, A. N., and Evans, J. G. (eds), *Care of the Elderly*, pp. 81–95.

Butcher, H., and Crosbie, D. (1977), *Pensioned Off – a Study of the Needs of Elderly People in Cleaton Moor* (York: University of York).

Butler, R. (1974), 'Successful aging and the role of the life review', *Journal of the American Geriatrics Society*, vol. XXII, no. 12, pp. 529–35.

CCETSW Paper 3 (1973), *Residential Work is a Part of Social Work* (London: Central Council for Education and Training in Social Work).

CCETSW Paper 9: 1 (1975), *A New Form of Training – the Certificate in Social Service* (London: Central Council for Education and Training in Social Work).

CCETSW (1978), *Abstracts of Data* and *CSS Schemes, Annual Student Intake* (London: Central Council for Education and Training in Social Work).

Canvin, R. W., and Pearson, N. G. (eds) (1973), *Needs of the Elderly for Health and Welfare Services* (Exeter: University of Exeter Institute of Biometry and Community Medicine).

Carter, K., and Evans, T. N. (1978), 'Intentions and achievements in admissions of the elderly to residential care', *Clearing House for Local Authority Social Services Research*, no. 9, pp. 71–99.

Challis, D., and Davies, B. (1980), 'A new approach to community care for the elderly', *British Journal of Social Work*, vol. 10, no. 1 (Spring), pp. 1–18.

Chapman, P. (1979), *Unmet Needs and the Delivery of Care*, Occasional Papers in Social Administration No. 61 (London: Bedford Square Press for Social Administration Research Trust).

CIPFA (1979), *Personal Social Services Statistics: 1977–78 Actuals* (London: Chartered Institute of Public Finances and Accountancy).

Consumer's Viewpoint (1978), 'An old folk's home', *Social Work Today*, vol. 9, no. 44 (18 July), p. 16.

Cormican, E. J. (1977), 'Task-centred model for work with the aged', *Social Casework* (October), pp. 490–4.

Coulshed, V. (1980), 'A unitary approach to the care of the hospitalised elderly mentally ill', *British Journal of Social Work*, vol. 10, no. 1 (Spring), pp. 19–32.

Court Report (1976), *Fit for the Future* (London: HMSO).

Cumming, E., and Henry, W. E. (1961), *Growing Old – The Process of Disengagement* (New York: Basic Books).

Cypher, J. (1977), 'Initial training?', *Community Care*, no. 171 (20 July), pp. 18–19.

DHSS (1973), *The Remedial Professions – Report by a Working Party* (London: HMSO).

DHSS (1976), *Priorities for Health and Personal Social Services in England – a*

Consultative Document (London: HMSO).
DHSS (1977), *The Way Forward* (London: HMSO).
DHSS (1978), *Social Service Teams: The Practitioner's View* (London: HMSO).
de Beauvoir, S. (1969), *A Very Easy Death* (first published 1964; English translation Harmondsworth: Penguin, 1969).
de Beauvoir, S. (1977), *Old Age* (London: Deutsch/Weidenfeld & Nicolson).
Digby, A. (1978), *Pauper Palaces* (London: Routledge & Kegan Paul).
Dunnachie, N. (1979), 'Intensive domiciliary care of the elderly in Hove', *Social Work Service*, no. 21 (November), pp. 1–3.
Eisdorfer, C. (1977), 'Mental health problems in the aged', in Exton-Smith, A. N., and Evans, J. G., (eds), *Care of the Elderly*, pp. 59–67.
Erikson, K. T. (1979), 'In the wake of the flood', *New Society* (10 May), pp. 326–7.
Exton-Smith, A. N., and Evans, J. G., (eds) (1977), *Care of the Elderly: Meeting the Challenge of Dependency* (London: Academic Press).
Fairhurst, E. (1977), *Teamwork as Panacea: Some Underlying Assumptions* (Manchester: Geigy Centre for Research in Ageing).
Fuller, J., Ward, E., Evans, A., Massam, K., and Gardner, A. (1979), 'Dementia: supportive groups for relatives', *British Medical Journal*, vol. 1 (23 June), pp. 1684–5.
Goffman, E. (1961), *Asylums* (New York: Anchor Books).
Going Home? (1975), Report on the Continuing Care Project of Age Concern Liverpool (Liverpool: Age Concern, 6 Stanley Street, Liverpool, L1 6AF).
Goldberg, E. M., Mortimer, A., and Wilhams, B. T. (1970), *Helping the Aged: A Field Experiment in Social Work* (London: Allen & Unwin).
Goldberg, E. M., and Neill, J. (1972), *Social Work in General Practice* (London: Allen & Unwin).
Goldberg, E. M., and Fruin, D. J. (1976), 'Towards accountability in social work: a case review system for social workers', *British Journal of Social Work*, vol. 6, no. 1, pp. 3–22.
Goldberg, E. M., and Connelly, N. (1978), 'Reviewing services for the old', *Community Care*, no. 242 (6 December), pp. 27–30.
Goldberg, E. M., Warburton, R. W., McGuiness, B., and Rowlands, J. H. (1977), 'Towards accountability in social work: one year's intake to an area office', *British Journal of Social Work*, vol. 7, no. 3, pp. 257–83.
Goldberg, E. M., Warburton, R. W., Lyons, L. J., and Willmott, R. R. (1978), 'Towards accountability in social work: long term social work in an area office', *British Journal of Social Work*, vol. 8, no. 3, pp. 253–88.
Gramlich, E. P. (1973), 'Recognition and management of grief in elderly patients', in Brantl, V. M., and Brown, M. P. (eds), *Readings in Gerontology*, pp. 105–10.
Gubrium, J. F. (ed.) (1976), *Time, Roles and Self in Old Age* (New York: Human Sciences Press).
Gunzburg, H. C., and Gunzburg, A. L. (1973), *Mental Handicap and Physical Environment: The Application of an Operational Philosophy to Planning* (London: Bailliere Tindall).
Gutman, G. M., and Herbert, C. P. (1977), in Hulicka, I. M. (ed.), *Empirical Studies in the Psychology and Sociology of Aging*, pp. 282–4.

Hadley, R., Webb, A., and Farrell, C. (1975), *Across the Generations* (London: Allen & Unwin).

Harris, P. B. (1979), 'Being old: a confrontation group with nursing home residents', *Health and Social Work*, vol. 4, no. 1, pp. 153–65.

Hill, M. J., and Laing, P. (1978), *Money Payments, Social Work and Supplementary Benefits: A Study of Section One of the 1963 Children and Young Persons' Act* (Bristol: University of Bristol School for Advanced Urban Studies, Occasional Paper No. 1).

Hill, M. J., and Laing, P. (1979), *Social Work and Money* (London: Allen & Unwin).

Holme, A., and Maizels, J. (1978), *Social Workers and Volunteers* (London: Allen & Unwin).

Hudson, B. (1978), 'Jack of all trades?', *Health and Social Service Journal*, vol. LXXXVIII, no. 4580, p. 251.

Hulicka, I. M. (ed.) (1977), *Empirical Studies in the Psychology and Sociology of Aging* (New York: Thomas Crowell).

Hunt, A. (1970), *The Home Help Service in England and Wales* (London: HMSO).

Hunt, A. (1978), *The Elderly at Home: A Study of People Aged Sixty-Five and Over Living in the Community in England in 1976*, Office of Population Censuses and Surveys (London: HMSO).

Isaacs, B. (1971), 'Geriatric patients: do their families care?', *British Medical Journal*, vol. 4, pp. 282–6.

Isaacs, B., and Neville, Y. (1976), *The Measurement of Need in Old People*, Scottish Health Service Studies No. 34 (Edinburgh: Scottish Home and Health Department).

Jay Report (1979), *Report of the Committee of Enquiry into Mental Handicap, Nursing and Care* (London: HMSO).

Kane, R. (1975), *Interprofessional Teamwork* (Syracuse, New York: Syracuse University School of Social Work).

Kay, D. W. K., Beamish, P., and Roth, M. (1964), 'Old age mental disorders in Newcastle-upon-Tyne. Part 1. A study of prevalence', *British Journal of Psychiatry*, vol. 110, pp. 146–58.

Kent Community Care Project (1979), *An Interim Report* (Canterbury: University of Kent at Canterbury, Personal Social Services Research Unit).

Kiley, M. (1977), 'The social worker's role in a nursing home', *Social Casework* (February), pp. 119–21.

Kirschner, C. (1979), 'The aging family in crisis', *Social Casework* (April), pp. 209–16.

Klein, M. (1959), 'Our adult world and its roots in infancy', *Human Relations*, vol. 12, pp. 291–303.

Kosberg, J. I., and Harris, A. P. (1978), 'Attitudes towards elderly clients', *Health and Social Work*, vol. 3, no. 3, pp. 67–90.

Kübler-Ross, E. (1969), *On Death and Dying* (London: Macmillan).

Layard, R., Piachaud, D., and Stewart, M. (1978), *The Causes of Poverty*, Royal Commission on the Distribution of Income and Wealth, Background Paper No. 5 (London: HMSO).

Leared, J. (1978), 'Bereavement and mourning', *Social Work Today*, vol. 9, no. 45 (25 July), pp. 16–17.

Lowther, C., and Williamson, J. (1966), 'Old people and their relatives', *Lancet* (31 December), pp. 1459–60.

Maiston, N., and Gupta, H. (1977), 'Interesting the old', *Community Care*, no. 188, pp. 26–8.

Marris, P. (1958), *Widows and Their Families* (London: Routledge & Kegan Paul).

Marris, P. (1974), *Loss and Change* (London: Routledge & Kegan Paul).

Marshall, M., and Boaden, N. (1978), 'Residential care: how can we make admission less haphazard?', *Modern Geriatrics* (January), pp. 30–3.

Martin, D., and Peckford, B. (1978), 'Hearing impairment in homes for the elderly', *Social Work Service*, no. 17 (October), pp. 52–62.

Mayer, J. E., and Timms, N. (1970), *The Client Speaks – Working Class Impressions of Casework* (London: Routledge & Kegan Paul).

Meacher, M. (1972), *Taken for a Ride* (London: Longman).

Menzies, I. E. P. (1960), 'A case study in the functioning of social systems as a defence against anxiety', *Human Relations*, vol. 13.

Mercer, S., and Kane, R. A. (1979), 'Helplessness and hopelessness amongst institutionalized aged: an experiment', *Health and Social Work*, vol. 4, no. 1 (February), pp. 91–116.

Miller, D., and Lieberman, M. A. (1965), 'The relationship of affect state and adaptive capacity to reactions to stress', *Journal of Gerontology*, vol. 20, pp. 492–7.

Mind Out (1978) (Journal of the National Association for Mental Health), no. 30 (September–October).

Mooney, G. H. (1978), 'Planning for balance of care of the elderly', *Scottish Journal of Political Economy*, vol. 25, no. 2 (June), pp. 149–64.

Moroney, R. M. (1976), *The Family and the State: Considerations for Social Policy* (London: Longman).

Morris, R. (1977), 'Caring for *vs* caring about people', *Social Work*, vol. 22 (September), pp. 353–9.

Newson, J. and Newson, E. (1968), *Four Years Old in an Urban Community* (London: Allen & Unwin).

Nolen, M. S., and Schaengold, M. (1978), 'Social work services in a long-term care facility', *Journal of Long-Term Care Administration*, vol. 6, pt 1, pp. 38–45.

Norman, A. J. (1980), *Rights and Risk: A Discussion Document on Civil Liberty in Old Age* (London: National Corporation for the Care of Old People).

Office of Health Economics (1979), *Dementia in Old Age* (London: Office of Health Economics).

Office of Population Censuses and Survey (OPCS) (1978), *Demographic Review* (London: HMSO).

Office of Population Censuses and Survey (1979), *Social Trends No. 8* (London: HMSO).

Opit, L. J. (1977), 'Domiciliary care for the elderly sick: economy or neglect?', *British Medical Journal*, vol. 1, pp. 30–3.

Parkes, C. M. (1972a), *Bereavement: Studies of Grief in Adult Life* (London: Tavistock).

Parkes, C. M. (1972b), 'Components of the reaction to loss of a limb, spouse or home', *Journal of Psychosomatic Research*, vol. 16, pp. 343–9.

Pattie, A. H., and Gilleard, C. J. (1978), 'Admission and adjustment of residents in homes for the elderly', *Journal of Epidemiology and Community Health*, vol. 32, pp. 212–14.

Payne, C. (1977), 'Residential social work' in Specht, H., and Vickery, A. (eds), *Integrating Social Work Methods* (London: Allen & Unwin), pp. 195–216.

Perlman, H. H. (1957), *Social Casework: A Problem Solving Process* (Chicago: University of Chicago Press).

Pincus, A. (1970), 'Reminiscence in aging and its implications for social work practice', *Social Work*, vol. 15, no. 3, pp. 47–53.

Pincus, A., and Minahan, A. (1973), *Social Work Practice: Model and Method* (Itasca, Ill.: Peacock).

Plank, D. (1977), *Caring for the Elderly: A Report of a Study of Various Means of Caring for Dependent Elderly People in 8 London Boroughs* (London: Greater London Council).

Pope, P. (1978), 'Admissions to residential homes for the elderly', *Social Work Today*, vol. 9, no. 44 (18 July), pp. 12–16.

Rapoport, R., and Rapoport, R. N., with Strelitz, Z. (1975), *Leisure and the Family Life Cycle* (London: Routledge & Kegan Paul).

Rapoport, R., Rapoport, R. N., and Strelitz, Z. (1977), *Fathers, Mothers and Others* (London: Routledge & Kegan Paul).

Reid, W. J., and Epstein, L. (1972), *Task Centred Casework* (New York: Columbia University Press).

Ricketts, R. (1978), 'Screening the old', *Community Care*, no. 231 (20 September), p. 23.

Ritchie, D. (1960), *Stroke: A Diary of Recovery* (London: Faber).

Robb, B. (1967), *Sans Everything: A Case to Answer* (London: Nelson).

Rochlin, G. (1965), *Griefs and Discontents: The Forces of Change* (Boston, Mass.: Little, Brown).

Roe, P., and Guillem, G. (1978), 'The need for medical supervision in homes', *Health and Social Service Journal*, vol. LXXXVIII, no. 4578 (10 February), pp. 168–9.

Rowlings, C. (1978), *Social Work with the Elderly: Some Problems and Possibilities* (Keele: University of Keele).

Sainsbury, E. (1975), *Social Work with Families* (London: Routledge & Kegan Paul).

Sainsbury, P., and Grad de Alarcon, J. (1971), 'The psychiatrist and the geriatric patient', *Journal of Geriatric Psychiatry*, vol. 14, pt I, pp. 23–4.

Sanford, J. R. A. (1975), 'Tolerance of debility in elderly dependants by supporters at home: its significance for hospital practice', *British Medical Journal*, vol. 3, pp. 471–3.

Shanas, E., Townsend, P., Wedderburn, D., Friis, H., Milhøj, P., and Stehouwer, J. (1968), *Old People in Three Industrial Societies* (London: Routledge & Kegan Paul).

Shanas, E., and Sussman, B. (eds) (1977), *Family, Bureaucracy and the Elderly* (Durham, NC: Duke University Press).

Shulman, K. (1978), 'Suicide and parasuicide in old age: a review', *Age and*

Ageing, vol. 7, pp. 201–9.

Simos, B. G. (1973), 'Adult children and their aging parents', *Social Work*, vol. 18, no. 3, pp. 78–85.

Simpson, R. (1979), *Access to Primary Care*, Royal Commission on the NHS, Research Paper No. 6 (London: HMSO).

Sinfield, A. (1969), *Which Way for Social Work?*, Fabian Tract 393 (London: Fabian Society).

Soyer, D. (1969), 'Reverie on working with the aged', *Social Casework*, vol. 14 (May), pp. 291–4.

Steinmetz, S. K. (1978), 'Battered parents', *Society*, vol. 15, pt 5, pp. 54–5.

Stockport Social Services Department (1978), papers concerning introduction of mobile warden scheme (Metropolitan Borough of Stockport, Social Services Division).

Streltzer, A. (1979), 'A grandchildren's group in a home for the aged', *Health and Social Work*, vol. 4, no. 1 (February), pp. 167–83.

Supplementary Benefits Commission (1979), *Annual Report for Year Ended 1978* (London: HMSO).

Tizard, B. (1977), *Adoption – A Second Chance* (London: Open Books).

Tobin, S. S., and Lieberman, M. A. (1976), *Last Home for the Aged* (San Francisco: Jossey-Bass).

Townsend, P. (1962), *The Last Refuge* (London: Routledge & Kegan Paul).

Tunstall, J. (1966), *Old and Alone* (London: Routledge & Kegan Paul).

Vickery, A. (1973), 'Specialist, generic, what next?', *Social Work Today*, vol. 4, no. 9 (26 July), pp. 262–6.

Vickery, A. (1977), *Caseload Management: A Guide for Supervisors of Social Work Staff* (London: National Institute for Social Work).

Wasser, E. (1966), *Creative Approaches in Casework with the Aging* (New York: Family Service Association of America).

Wasser, E. (1971), 'Protective practice in serving the mentally impaired aged', *Social Casework*, vol. 52, no. 8, pp. 510–22.

Weiner, M. B., Brok, A. J., and Snadowsky, A. M. (1978), *Working with the Aged: Practical Approaches in the Institution and Community* (Englewood Cliffs, NJ: Prentice-Hall).

Wicke, M. (1978), 'Time to go home', *New Age*, vol. 3 (Summer), pp. 20–1.

Wilkin, D., and Jolley, D. (1978), *Behavioural Problems among Old People in Geriatric Wards, Psychogeriatric Wards and Residential Homes* (Manchester: University Hospital of South Manchester, Psychogeriatric Unit – Research Section).

Williams Report (1967), *Caring for People: Staffing Residential Homes* (London: Allen & Unwin).

Williamson, J., Stokoe, I. H., Gray, S., Fisher, M., Smith, A., McGhee, A., and Stephenson, E. (1964), 'Old people at home: their unreported needs', *Lancet*, vol. 23 (May), pp. 1117–20.

Winnicott, C. (1964), *Child Care and Social Work* (Hitchin, Herts: The Codicote Press).

Wootton, B. (1959), *Social Science and Social Pathology* (London: Allen & Unwin).

Worth, D. (1975), 'I'm not poor, I'm not old and I'm not her dear', *Community Care* (17 December), pp. 12–13.

Yawney, B. A., and Slover, D. L. (1973), 'Relocation of the elderly', *Social Work* (New York), vol. 18, no. 3, pp. 86–95.

Younghusband, E. (1964), *Social Work and Social Change* (London: Allen & Unwin).

Index